THE CIVILIZATION OF THE AMERICAN INDIAN SERIES

DRESS CLOTHING
OF THE PLAINS INDIANS

Figure 1. Crow Encampment. Painting by Alfred Jacob Miller, 1837. Courtesy of t Walters Art Gallery, Baltimore, Maryland.

Dress Clothing of the Plains Indians

by Ronald P. Koch

UNIVERSITY OF OKLAHOMA PRESS : NORMAN

Library of Congress Cataloging-in-Publication Data

Koch, Ronald Peter, 1932-
  Dress clothing of the Plains Indians.

  (The Civilization of the American Indian series; 140)
  Bibliography: p. 201
  Includes index.
  1. Indians of North America—Great Plains—Costume
and adornment. I. Title. II. Series.
E78.G73K6   391   76-46947

  ISBN: 0–8061–1372–3
  ISBN: 0–8061–2137–8 (pbk.)

7 8 9 10 11 12 13 14 15 16 17 18

This publication is respectfully dedicated to the memory of Ellsworth Jaeger, *the "Chief" to many of us who were his friends.*

FOREWORD AND
ACKNOWLEDGMENTS

The American Indian, and particularly the tribes living on the Great Plains of the North American continent, have long aroused the interest of people in other lands and of other cultural backgrounds. This enthusiasm was reflected in Thomas Jefferson's creation of the Lewis and Clark Expedition. George Catlin's gallery of paintings drew crowds of thousands when it toured the European continent. Even today, many visitors throng to the fairs, rodeos, dances, and powwows of Plains tribes each summer.

Perhaps part of the fascination lies in the costumes worn on dress occasions, with their colorful display of painted, quilled, and beaded designs; rhythmic movement of feathers and furs; and plethora of sounds of bells, shells, beads, and metals.

To the uninitiated, this clothing may all seem quite similar, and, indeed, some early travelers on the Plains described clothing as typical of the whole region. Careful study shows, however, that there were, and are, distinct differences from tribe to tribe, north to south, east to west. As in other cultural traits, such as thoughts about death, treatment of visitors, and the like, clothing reveals the Plains as a multifaceted culture area.

The present work can be considered a "primer" for those wishing to acquaint themselves more with this Plains costume heritage—the casual powwow visitor, the hobbyist, the American Indian himself. Clothing is separated out by time and place, for men and women.

Better answers can be found in more advanced sources; the reader can find more information by studying the work of early artists such as Catlin and Carl Bodmer, early photographs, and, for costumes of the present day, by visiting the many Indian activities held each year.

The major separation in the text is by materials used and clothing parts, rather than by geography. As can be said for the clothing of any people, if a material can be used, it is used, most certainly so if you feel the material adds aesthetically to your appearance or is more comfortable in your area. Hence, there were fur-lined boots on the northern Plains in the winter; high-top boots on the southern Plains to protect the legs from travel through brush.

Useful introductions from Europe were seized upon rapidly. The horse radically changed life on the Plains. Beads, metals, cloth — all were rapidly assimilated in Plains clothing ornamentation.

Of necessity, only a sampling of a large field of study is presented. Without doubt, one person could spend a lifetime of study on a subject such as Plains hair ornaments or dress clothing of the Northern Cheyennes. The trend is toward a presentation of the most common apparel for the most common dances and ceremonies. Some items—breechcloths, for example—are so rare in museum collections, old photographs, and paintings and writings of those who made early contacts with the Plains people that treatment is very general and superficial. A slight leaning toward men's clothing occurs for the same reason, rather than as a result of male chauvinism.

First and foremost, I wish to acknowledge the efforts of my wife, Loraine, whose patience and occasional prodding were extremely beneficial. Rosemary and F. Dennis Lessard, of the Del Trading Post, were very helpful in reading several drafts of the manuscript and offering many critical comments concerning necessary additions and deletions; dozens of letters back and forth really polished this work into its final form.

Mrs. Esther Olczak typed the original material. A young artist friend, Robert Spengler, Jr., spent many hours in preparing the India-ink illustrations incorporated in the book, his only compensation being the development of his personal artistic skills.

In a book such as this, which brings together the ideas of many persons concerning a particular subject area, the plethora of informants must be thanked as a group. Apology is offered for errors which may have been unknowingly committed, and sincere appreciation is extended for the wealth of material provided by many students of Plains Indian clothing who have published their findings in the literature available to the writer. Last, but not least, thanks are due the staff of the University of Oklahoma Press; the editors have provided many helpful suggestions concerning style and content.

RONALD P. KOCH

Depew, New York

CONTENTS

ILLUSTRATIONS

DRESS CLOTHING
OF THE PLAINS INDIANS

Figure 2. People of the Plains. The map indicates the approximate location of tribes about 1835.

1. THE PEOPLE OF THE PLAINS

To introduce the text properly, the reader should know the tribes to be highlighted and the time periods involved. If we go way back, we learn that very few tribes lived on the Plains: a few farmers on the eastern fringe; hunters on the west, happy with a small take from the huge herds of bison. We can only dream of what might have happened had this situation not been changed. Perhaps a high form of culture might have come with the passage of time among the sedentary agricultural groups in the east; some historians seem to press the idea that great civilizations spring from farming people with crop surpluses. The fact remains that the horse, introduced (perhaps, for the vertebrate paleontologist, we should say reintroduced) by the Spaniards to the New World, had dramatic effects on the Plains, even before any white man was to be found there.[1]

The doom of the bison was inevitable (with or without white hunters). People migrated onto the Plains (1700–1850), and a new form of life developed. The introduction of the horse was not the only reason for migration to the Plains; population pressure from the East and the lure of the abundant food basket of the Plains were also very important factors.

The new life on the Plains brought changes in costuming. As just one example of such changes, the "war bonnet," which was difficult to wear in a forested area, arose among either the Sioux or the Crows on the Plains, spreading rapidly to other tribesmen. This

3

bonnet, said to be symbolic of the sun and its spreading rays, was originally very uncommon; it could be worn only by the bravest of the brave. To those purists who say that these bonnets belong only with Sioux costuming, the reply should be, "When?" If an early time is meant, it could be said the Sioux didn't use these bonnets. A few decades later, the Sioux wore them. A few years later, bonnets cap the bravest warriors of every Plains tribe. In modern times, thanks to the glamorizing of the Sioux, every important Indian, no matter where he lives, is expected to own and wear a war bonnet.

Tribes to be named in the text are indicated on the map, "People of the Plains" (Figure 2). Some could more properly be called Prairie tribes; others, Plateau tribes.

> Today these [Plateau] Indians exhibit many Plains culture elements, but most of these elements have reached them within the last century and a half. Their aboriginal culture was quite distinct from that of the Plains. . . . Much of Plains culture stemmed directly from that of the Prairies. Nevertheless, the Prairie area also shows many ties with the East and appears to be culturally transitional between the two.[2]

Lacking a dividing ocean, we must never conceive of any culture area, such as the Plains, as a region with a wall around it. This will become particularly apparent as trade is discussed. "Plains costumes, dances and songs are still being acquired by Indians whose cultures in prehistoric times were very different."[3]

In like manner, ". . . it is clear that scarcely a single important feature of a given garment is peculiar to a single tribe but that two or more in geographical continuity share it equally. It also appears that the more fundamental a given feature, the wider its distribution."[4]

Ancestral ties such as existed between Crows and Hidatsas contributed to the sharing of costume ideas. Inamicability, for example between the neighboring Blackfoot and Plains Cree tribes, slowed such an exchange.

> Plains clothing varies greatly in degree of ornamentation from south to north. Southern Plains clothing is marked by an

almost complete lack of any type of decoration except fringing. The use of fringes of all types is highly developed among the southern tribes of the area and reaches its peak in the twisted variety, the finest made and most attractive looking of all fringe types.

On the northern Plains, on the other hand, many elaborate types of clothing decoration were the rule. These are bead and quill embroidery, the use of human and animal hair and white fur; and of feathers.

Paint was used throughout the Plains area. Solid colors seem to have predominated in the South, while detailed designs, both abstract and more or less realistic, appear to have been more frequent in the central and northern sections. Another generally used type of decoration, the tin jingler, was more common in the South.

The tribes of the central Plains occupied a middle ground in the matter of decoration and used plain or elaborate types according to their position in relation to the North or South.[5]

Figure 3. Prairie chickens. The hen is on the left; the male, on the right.

2. FEATHERS

The first step in analyzing the costumes of any group of people must be a study of the materials which were available for use, as well as a description, in elementary terms, of techniques for their use and something of the designs employed. Materials have rather arbitrarily been divided into three categories: (1) native materials other than skins, i.e., materials used before the period of European influence; (2) trade materials introduced by whites, the separation here obviously being historical; and (3) use of whole animal skins.

Before the introduction of colorful modern dyes, brightness was much sought after. Aborigines of many countries found desired colors in the plumage and pelts of birds. The Jivaros and other South American jungle tribes to this day make extensive use of avian plumage for clothing and ornamentation. So it was on the Plains; the bright feathers even of macaws and parrots found their way by hand-to-hand trading thousands of miles to Plains tribesmen.

Local birds were more common as a source of colorful feathers—scissortails, road runners, orioles, flickers and various other woodpeckers, ducks and swans, water turkeys, and yellow-headed blackbirds—the plumage of all has been reported as having been used in Plains costumes.

Turkeys and prairie chickens (Figure 3) furnished an abundance of plumage for decorative purposes. As will be mentioned later, quills from gulls and other birds were sometimes used instead of porcupine quills in Plains quillwork. Ravens, crows, and magpies

7

(a western relative of the crow) were very common; their black feathers were often used in headdresses, especially in the societies of certain Plains tribes. Edwin Denig reported that crow-skin head-dresses were worn by young warriors, while owl feathers were worn by new beginners.[1]

> The crow (ho) is the sacred bird of the Ghost dance. . . . The raven, which is practically a larger crow, and which lives in the mountains, but occasionally comes down into the plains, is also held sacred and regarded as a bringer of omens by the prairie tribes. . . . The crow is depicted on the shirts, leggings, and moccasins of the Ghost dancers, and its feathers are worn on their heads, and whenever it is possible to kill one, the skin is stuffed as in life and carried in the [Ghost] dance. . . . The crow was probably held sacred by all the tribes of the Algonquian race [linguistic stock].[2]

Birds of prey have long been held in awe by men of many areas. Feathers of sparrow hawks, hawks, owls, and especially of bald and golden eagles found frequent use in costuming. Kroeber describes a dog-dancer shirt covered with crow feathers, and depicts a dog-dancer headdress of owl feathers. Use of owl feathers in the Crazy-dance regalia is also cited. According to Fletcher and LaFlesche, among the Osages, "The wa-xo-be, made of the skin of a hawk, is a symbol of courage, and is carried by a commanding officer on his back when leading his men in an attack."[3]

The pheasant was introduced into Oregon in the 1880's and rapidly spread its territory. Individual feathers, as well as full skins, soon found their way into Plains Indian clothing. They became especially popular in bustles.

Wherever found, the eagle was regarded as sacred among the Indian tribes both east and west, and its feathers were highly prized for ornamental and "medicine" purposes, and an elaborately detailed ritual of prayer and ceremony was the necessary accompaniment to its capture. Among all the tribes the chief purpose of this ritual was to obtain the help of the gods in inducing the eagle to approach the hunter, and to turn aside the anger of the eagle spirits at the necessary sacrilege. The feathers most valued were those of the tail and wings. These were used to ornament lances and shields, to wear upon the head, and to decorate the magnificent war bonnets, the finest of which have a pendant or trail of eagle-tail feathers reaching from the warrior's head to the ground when he stands erect. The whistle used in the sun dance and other great ceremonies is made of a bone from the leg or wing of the eagle, and the fans carried by the warriors on parade and used also to sprinkle the holy water in the mescal ceremony of the southern prairie tribes is commonly made of the entire tail or wing of that bird. Hawk feathers are sometimes used for these purposes, but are always considered far inferior to those of the eagle. . . . The eagle-feather war bonnets and eagle-tail fans are the most valuable parts of an Indian's outfit and the most difficult to purchase from him. . . . Among the prairie tribes along the whole extent of the plains [eagles] were never shot, but must be captured alive in pitfalls and then strangled or crushed to death, if possible without the shedding of blood. A description of the Arapaho method will answer with slight modifications for all the prairie tribes.

The hunter withdrew with his family away from the main camp to some rough hilly country where the eagles were abundant. After some preliminary prayers he went alone to the top of the highest hill and there dug a pit large enough to sit or lie down in, being careful to carry the earth taken out of the hole so far away from the place that it would not attract the notice of the eagle. The pit was roofed over with a covering of light willow twigs, above which were placed earth and grass to give it a natural appearance. The bait was a piece of fresh meat, or a piece of tallow stripped from the ribs of the buffalo. This was tied to a rawhide string and laid upon the top of the pit, while the rope was passed down through the roof into the cavity below. A coyote skin, stuffed and set up erect as in life, was sometimes placed near the bait to add to the realistic effect.

Having sat up all night, singing the eagle songs and purifying himself for the ceremony, the hunter started before daylight, without eating any breakfast or drinking water, and went up the hill to the pit, which he entered, and, having closed the opening, he seated himself inside holding the end of the string in his hands, to prevent a coyote or other animal from taking the bait, and waiting for the eagles to come.

Should other birds come, he drove them away or paid no attention to them. When at last the eagle came the other birds at once flew away. The eagle swooped down, alighting always at one side and then walking over upon the roof of the trap to get at the bait, when the hunter, putting up his hand through the framework, seized the eagle by the legs, pulled it down and quickly strangled it or broke its neck. He then rearranged the bait and the roof and sat down to wait for another eagle. He might be so lucky as to capture several during the day, or so unfortunate as to take none at all. At night, but not before, he repaired to his own tipi to eat, drink, and sleep, and was at the pit again before daylight. While in the pit he did not eat, drink, or sleep. The eagle hunt, if it may be so called, lasted four days, and must end then, whatever might have been the good or bad fortune of the hunter.

At the expiration of four days he returned to his home with the dead bodies of the eagles thus caught. A small lodge was set up outside his tipi and in this the eagles were hung up by the neck upon the pole laid across two forked sticks driven into the ground. After some further prayers and purifications the feathers were stripped from the bodies as they hung.[4]

Rather than repeat directions for preparing feathers (eagle or imitation eagle) for use, the reader is referred to popular craft books.[5] Several things should be pointed out, however. Use of colored (dyed) feathers, cutting of plumes, use of fluffies, horsehair, or leather circles at the tip, and use of fluffies at the base varied from tribe to tribe. In comparing the Gros Ventres with the Arapahoes, for example, Kroeber said:

The Gros Ventre rarely ornament their feather with dyed fluffies of tufts of horsehair, as the Arapaho so frequently do both at the base and top of the feather. Feathers with the web cut from the quill, except at the very top, are also scarcely used by the Gros Ventre. Instead, they usually cut the feather squarely off across its end, or split the quill, from the end down, for the greater part of its length. Sometimes the uppermost part of the quill is entirely removed, with its attached web portions, leaving the top of the feather forked. In dyeing, the Gros Ventre generally used cruder colors; a blue-violet, a pink-red, a light bluish green, and yellow, all of them aniline colors, being the most common. The Arapaho use true red and green more frequently, and in most cases employ the dyes more lightly, thus obtaining endurable or delicate effects where the Gros Ventre are garish.

The Gros Ventre methods of feather-treatment, both the cutting-off and the splitting of the end of the feather, go back, at least in part, to their older tribal ceremonies.[6]

The base of the quill could be prepared for attachment either by fastening a leather strip to it or by cutting away half the quill to form a "pen," bending the "pen" over and slipping it into the hollow quill center (older method). For glue the Indian prepared a mucilage from native materials.

Each part of the preparation of a single feather might, in a certain tribe, have significance. In one tribe, for example, horsehair tips indicated the killing of an enemy.

Among the Plains Crees, the removal of web from most of the quill, with the exception of a small tuft at the end, indicated that the wearer had wrestled and overcome an enemy.[7]

Garrick Mallery assembled and presented the reports of several observers:

Prince Maximilian of Wied gives an account (as follows):

"The Sioux highly prize personal bravery, and therefore constantly wear the marks of distinction which they have received for their exploits; among these are, especially, tufts of

11

human hair attached to the arms and legs, and feathers on their heads. He who, in the sight of the adversaries, touches a slain or living enemy places a feather horizontally in his hair for this exploit.

"They look upon this as a very distinguished act, for many are killed in the attempt before the object is attained. He who kills an enemy by a blow with his fist sticks a feather upright in his hair.

"If the enemy is killed with a musket a small piece of wood is put in the hair, which is intended to represent a ramrod. If a warrior is distinguished by many deeds he has a right to wear the great feathercap with ox-horns. This cap, composed of eagle feathers, which are fastened to a long strip of red cloth hanging down the back, is highly valued by all the tribes on the Missouri. . . . Whoever first discovers the enemy and gives notice to his comrades of their approach is allowed to wear a small feather which is stripped except towards the top."

The following scheme, used by the Dakotas [Sioux], is taken from Mrs. Eastman's *Dahcotah*. Colors are not given, but red undoubtedly predominates, as is known from [Mallery's] personal observation [Figure 4].

[A shows] a spot upon the larger web [which] denotes that the wearer has killed an enemy.

[B] denotes that the wearer has cut the throat of his enemy and taken his scalp.

[C] denotes that the wearer has cut the throat of his enemy.

[D] denotes that the wearer was the third that touched the body of his enemy after he was killed.

[E] denotes that the wearer was the fourth that touched the body of his enemy after he was killed.

[F] denotes that the wearer was the fifth that touched the body of his enemy after he was killed.

[G] denotes that the wearer has been wounded in many places by the enemy.

The following variations in the scheme were noticed in

Figure 4. Feather symbolism. Adapted from Garrick Mallery, "Picture-Writing of the American Indians," Smithsonian Institution, Bureau of American Ethnology *Tenth Annual Report, 1888–1889* (1893).

1883 among the Mdewakantanwan Dakotas, near Fort Snelling, Minnesota.

Feathers of the eagle are used as among the other bands of Dakotas.

A plain feather is used to signify that the wearer has killed an enemy, without regard to the manner in which he was slain.

When the end is clipped transversely, and the edge colored red, it signifies that the throat of the enemy was cut.

A black feather denotes that an Ojibwa woman was killed. Enemies are considered as Ojibwas, that being the tribe with which the Mdewakantanwan Dakotas have been most in collision.

When a warrior has been wounded a red spot is painted upon the broad side of a feather. If the wearer has been shot in the body, arms, or legs, a red spot is painted upon his clothing or blanket, immediately over the locality of the wound. These red spots are sometimes worked in porcupine quills, or in cotton fiber as now obtained from the traders.

Belden . . . says:

"Among the Sioux an eagle's feather with a red spot painted on it, worn by a warrior in the village, denotes that on the last war-path he killed an enemy, and for every additional enemy he has slain he carries another feather painted with an additional red spot about the size of a silver quarter.

"A red hand painted on a warrior's blanket denotes that he has been wounded by the enemy, and a black one that he has been unfortunate in some way."

Boller . . . describes a Sioux as wearing a number of small wood shavings stained with vermilion in his hair, each the symbol of a wound received.

Lynd . . . gives a device differing from all the foregoing, with an explanation:

"To the human body the Dakotas give four spirits. The first is supposed to be a spirit of the body, and dies with the body. The second is a spirit which always remains with or near the body. Another is the soul which accounts for the deeds of the body, and is supposed by some to go to the south, by others to

14

the west, after the death of the body. The fourth always lingers with the small bundle of the hair of the deceased kept by the relatives until they have a chance to throw it into the enemy's country, when it becomes a roving, restless spirit, bringing death and disease to the enemy whose country it is in.

"From this belief arose the practice of wearing four scalp-feathers for each enemy slain in battle, one for each soul."

It should be noted that all the foregoing signs of individual achievements are given by the several authorities as used by the same body of Indians, the Dakota or Sioux. This, however, is a large body, divided into tribes, and it is possible that a different scheme was used in the several tribes. But the accounts are so conflicting that error in either observation or description or both is to be suspected.[8]

To diverge from Mallery for a moment, it should be stated that each account is probably right and that, if ten more observers had asked ten more individuals what their feathers "meant," they would probably have received ten more different interpretations. Feathers had meaning in prereservation days, but it was highly individualistic and varied greatly historically and geographically. There was no set "language of the feathers" for all tribes at all times.
Continuing from Mallery:

Prince Maximilian, of Wied . . ., thus reports on the designations of the Mandans connected with the present topic:

"The Mandans wear the large horned feather cap; this is a cap consisting of strips of white ermine with pieces of red cloth hanging down behind as far as the calves of the legs, to which is attached an upright row of black and white eagle feathers, beginning at the head and reaching to the whole length. Only distinguished warriors who have performed many exploits may wear this headdress.

"If the Mandans give away one or more of these headdresses, which they estimate very highly, they are immediately considered men of great importance. . . . On their buffalo robes

15

they often represent this feather cap under the image of a sun. Very celebrated and eminent warriors, when most highly decorated, wear in their hair various pieces of wood as signals of their wounds and heroic deeds. Thus Mato-Tope had fastened transversely in his hair a wooden knife painted red and about the length of a hand, because he had killed a Cheyenne chief with his knife; then six wooden sticks, painted red, blue, and yellow, with a brass nail at one end, indicating so many musket wounds which he had received. For an arrow wound he fastened in his hair the wing feather of a wild turkey; at the back of his head he wore a large bunch of owl's feathers, dyed yellow, with red tips, as the badge of the Meniss-Ochata (the dog band). The half of his face was painted red and the other yellow; his body was painted reddish-brown, with narrow stripes, which were produced by taking off the color with the tip of the finger wetted. On his arms, from the shoulder downwards, he had seventeen yellow stripes, which indicated his war-like deeds, and on his breast the figure of a hand, of a yellow color, as a sign that he had captured some prisoners. . . ."

The Hidatsa scheme of designating achievements was obtained by Dr. Hoffman, at Fort Berthold, North Dakota, during 1881, and now follows [Figure 4]:

[H.] A feather, to the tip of which is attached a tuft of down or several strands of horsehair, dyed red, denotes that the wearer has killed an enemy and that he was the first to touch or strike him with the coups stick. . . .

[I.] A feather bearing one red bar made with vermilion, signifies the wearer to have been the second person to strike the fallen enemy with the coup stick. . . .

[J.] A feather bearing two red bars signifies that the wearer was the third person to strike the body. . . .

[K.] A feather with three bars signifies that the wearer was the fourth to strike the fallen enemy. . . . Beyond this number honors are not counted.

[L.] A red feather denotes that the wearer was wounded in an encounter with an enemy. . . .

[M.] A narrow strip of rawhide or buckskin is wrapped from

16

end to end with porcupine quills dyed red, though sometimes a few white ones are inserted to break the monotony of color. This strip is attached to the inner surface of the quill by means of very thin fibers of sinew, and signifies that the wearer killed a woman belonging to a hostile tribe. . . . In very fine specimens the porcupine quills are directly applied to the feather quill without resorting to the strip of leather.

Similar marks denoting exploits are used by the Hidatsa, Mandan, and Arikara Indians. The Hidatsa claim to have been the originators of the devices.[8]

W. J. McGee quotes Buffalo Chief as saying that, among the Poncas:

Eagle feathers alone are used.

Feathers set upright on the crown indicate Captors (in battle), one feather being worn for each capture.

Feathers on the crown inclined (say 30 or 40 degrees) toward the right indicate Scalpers, i.e., such a feather indicates that the wearer has taken one or more scalps.

Feathers set low on the head and inclined toward the left indicate Leaders, or men who have achieved power and control through prowess in battle or in marauding expeditions.

Feathers stripped nearly to the top (i.e., to the black tip) and then broken so that the tip may wave and flutter in the wind indicate Finders, or courageous and successful scouts and ready lieutenants who succeed in discovering many houses (i.e., enemies, the black tip symbolizing the smoke-blackened house-tops). Such feathers are commonly worn upright on the crown, but the meaning is the same when attached to the clothing or to the mane or tail of the horse.

Eagle down is worn by shamans to indicate mysterious power, or control by the Mysteries; it is considered to render the wearer alert and swift, and to make him invisible to enemies and invulnerable to arrow and tomahawk. Soft, floating or waving down is the symbol of the "ghost" or "Mystery."

A baton or staff is carried by a man who has been wounded

17

in battle, or who has made narrow escapes, and is painted yellow, red, black, or variegated to correspond with the painting of the warrior at the time of his wound or escape; it confers power and authority on its bearer. A pendant feather attached to the baton signifies wounds, and increases the potency of the symbol.

The device (roach spreader) used for attaching the feather or feathers is significant, partly because [it is] archaic and hence sacred, partly because it contributes toward interpreting objects of unknown or doubtful purpose found in mounds and other tombs.[9]

Individual feathers could be worn in the hair or on a headpiece. Lewis and Clark noted, among the Sioux, hawk or eagle feathers worked with quills fastened to the top of the head. Perhaps this refers to ornamentation similar to that described earlier, originally made entirely of porcupine quills, but since around 1800, of horsehair and quills. Fine quills, of varied colors, were flattened and laid along a narrow strip of rawhide (or cane or ash splint). Individual horsehairs were wound round and round the rawhide, much as one would "whip" the end of a rope. Where desired, the horsehair was slipped under the quill, the quills thereby forming a design. New hairs were added merely by twisting a new hair to the end of the old and covering the splice with added turns of hair. These decorated thongs were sewed onto the feather quill, often with ermine strips or clusters of fluffs at the ends. Feathers decorated in this manner were used individually, in turbans and roaches, in fans, and in bustle spike feathers, especially by Prairie tribes.[10]

Fans could be made of a wing of the eagle, or an eagle tail, often with a strip of skin from the eagle back connecting the tail to the beaked head, which was left attached. The handle portion was often wrapped with cloth (strouding or a "kerchief"), and sometimes this was beaded or ribbon-appliqued. Wing fans were sometimes connected with specific religious ceremonies. Feather-quill ornaments were common on fans. A typical arrangement of these on tail fans was attachment to three underside feathers and to one top feather. Pawnee men carried a fan of goose or turkey feathers.[11]

Bustles appear to be a more recent use of feathers in costumes:

> Among the Omaha and other plains tribes men who had won high war honors were permitted to wear a feather decoration known as "the Crow" or "the Raven." By white men it is often called a dance bustle. . . . "The Crow" was worn at the back, being held in place by a belt of buckskin. It consisted of a rawhide frame covered with the entire skin of an eagle and from which two buckskin pendants hung down the wearer's legs, like the trail of a war bonnet. Projecting from it were two upright feather shafts tipped with red horsehair (doesn't have to be red and is rarely horsehair, more often being made from bull tail). Fur, loose feathers, and entire birdskins were often used on it as further decorations. "The Crow" symbolized a battlefield and only the feathers of birds that appeared after a battle were used in its construction. It took its name from an entire crowskin, which in the old days was one of its important parts, because the keen scent of this bird brought it to the battlefield before any of the others. Feathers of buzzards, magpies, and eagles were used because they were the second, third, and fourth birds to arrive. The eagle was also associated with war and the power of the thunder. The two upright shafts symbolized slain warriors and the arrows that had killed them. The one on the left represented an enemy and the one on the right a friend. In modern times this old symbolism has been forgotten, so that feathers of all sorts, together with decorations furnished by the traders, go into the making of a "Crow."[12]

The "uprights" were probably horizontal spikes in earlier years. The central birdskin was replaced about 1890 by a rosette made of several flat circles of feathers; the central ornament in this rosette was a mirror (beaded rosette later). About 1930, the trailers were sometimes left off and often the spikes, leaving only the circle of feathers. All kinds of long feathers can be used in the modern bustle; use of pheasant feathers was mentioned earlier, for example.

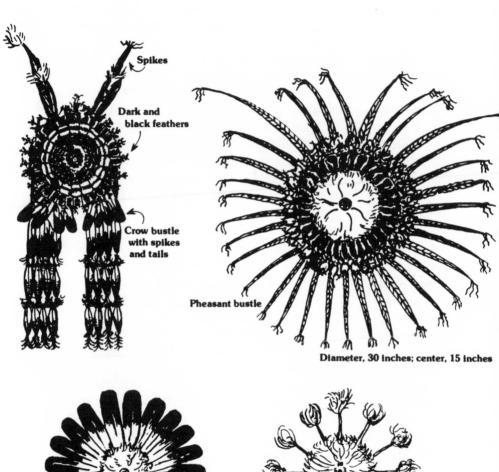

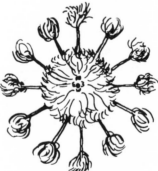

Figure 5. Bustle styles. Adapted from Bernard S. Mason, *The Book of Indian Crafts and Costumes* (New York, Ronald, 1946).

Buckskin trailers were soon replaced by blue stroud trailers. These early cloth trailers were covered with small eagle-wing feathers, the white selvage sometimes being cut in zig-zag fashion to ornament the bottom of the trailer. Modern Oklahoma trailers are much simpler, with just a couple of feathers or ribbons attached, frequently from beaded rosette centers. Occasionally one can also observe a single narrow trailer, simply ornamented. A single wide trailer is now used on the Plateau, with many variations in decoration.[13]

The bustle may have originated in the Middle West, and the important part was the belt rather than the decoration on it.[14] Bustles were an important part of the *Iruska* ceremony of the Pawnees, which is the probable progenitor of the Omaha, or Grass, Dance; this dance and the "crow," "belt," or "bustle" are intimately related.

Feather rosettes worn at the back of the neck, at the sides of the head (more common on the northern Plains), or on the forehead are rather modern. Old Flathead photographs indicate that dancers of this tribe sometimes wore feather rosettes at the back of the head (rather than neck). Feather rosettes on the elbows are uncommon, as they are a hindrance to the dancer.

Stuffed whole bird skins were often attached to costume pieces or formed part of the medicine bundle.

Use of feathers in legging fringes is shown by Catlin for the Mandans, the Otos, and the Omahas. Probably other tribes made a similar use of feathers. Sioux women wore a feather after the puberty rite and feathers in scalp dances at times. Mari Sandoz tells of a woman warrior using her brother's regalia, presumably including feathers.[15]

3. COLOR AND PAINTED DESIGNS

As was previously pointed out, colorful objects were highly valued in costuming. Objects lacking color were sometimes treated to supply this missing ingredient. Color was applied to bison-hide robes, shirts, leggings, and dresses, and later to blankets and cloth shirts. Color could be applied as a paint, as a dye, or as a stain. Paints consisted of solids suspended in a liquid or semiliquid medium. Dyes were prepared from organic materials in aqueous solution. Stains, as used here, refer to dyes or pigments applied only to one surface of a material. Animal hair, feathers, and porcupine quills were dyed. Paint, in addition to being used on clothing and other articles, was also applied to a person's face and, if exposed, the body itself, and often to the horses of a war party. In some areas, tattooing was also occasionally practiced, at least in an earlier period.

Red is generally accepted as being one of the colors most easily available to and most used by Indians. Yellow and blue (and/or blue black, remembering that a jet black was rather difficult to obtain) ran close seconds. Green and brown were favored by some tribes, not by others. White was used in relation to particular ceremonial occasions. After their introduction by traders, vivid oranges and purples were used, but infrequently. Similar color preferences were observed as dyestuff and, later, beads were introduced on the Plains.

Among some tribes, symbolic meaning was sometimes attached to particular colors, this symbolism varying from tribe to tribe. Red often referred to blood and, from this, to battle or to life itself. Yellow

23

could symbolize the sun, and, therefore, daytime. Light blue might be sky or a body of water, while dark blue might represent mountains or victory. Green most often symbolized vegetation, and brown, the earth, or animal life. Black might be thought of as the night or war; white, snow, winter, or—as in our own culture—purity or cleanliness.[1] Red Bird, a Sioux Sun Dancer, said that each color had

> a symbolism connected with the sky. Thus, it was said that red corresponds to the red clouds of sunset, which indicates fair weather; blue represents the cloudless sky; yellow, the forked lightning; white corresponds to the light; and black was used for everything associated with night, even the moon being painted black because it belonged to the hours of darkness.[2]

Again, it should be stressed that color symbolism was probably about as well known to the individual Indian as the symbolism of his own country's national colors is known to a person today. To carry this comparison still further, each nation, even today, may have color interpretations entirely alien to another nation bearing similar colors.

Roland Dixon, in discussing colors of the cardinal points, made several observations: (1) Different words did not exist for blue and black among some tribes; this sometimes was also true for green and blue among other tribes. (2) Colors chosen for directions might be exactly opposite for tribes of the same stock living near each other and be identical among widely separated groups. (3) A statistically common choice in the Plains area would be: north represented by blue or black; east, red; south, white; and west, red. (4) Local religious ideas had a major effect in determining the color choices.[3]

Sources of colors varied with locality. For stains and dyestuffs, organically derived materials were usually used. Red might be obtained from the bark of red osier dogwood, alder bark, buffalo berries, squaw currants, Viburnum drupes, wild-plum fruits, or bloodroot. Among some tribes tamarack bark, spruce cones, and sumac fruits yielded reds. Yellow came from wolf moss (fox moss, *Evernia vulpina*), sumac pith or roots, goldthread roots, certain lichens, early cottonwood buds, sunflower of coneflower petals (boiled with decayed oak bark or cattail roots), various parts of the female curled dock, buffalo berries, or the roots of black willow. Black was derived from black-walnut nuts or roots, butternuts, hazel burs, hickory nuts, maple bark and leaves, or wild grapes; the last were considered superior for dyeing. Possible sources of green included either green pond scum or grass. Green "took" better on some materials than on others. Brown might be derived from the same sources as black. "Dark brown, not black, paint . . . is a natural earth pigment widely traded throughout the Plains. It was generally found along the edges of peat bogs or at the bottom of stagnant ponds [and] . . . is probably a brown limonite. . . ."[4] John Ewers reports a "blue-colored plant" (larkspur, perhaps) as a source of blue;[5] blue was rare among many tribes before trade blankets were introduced. Light violet sometimes was derived from rotten maple wood, or from blueberries; light orange, from dodder vines.

Paints were usually inorganically derived. White, brown, red, yellow, and sometimes black clays were used. Mud, charcoal, or gunpowder produced black. Green and blue may have been obtained from copper ores or from clays, but their early use is questioned. As early as 1776, Chinese vermilion was being traded with the Assiniboins, although Indians had native sources of this pigment, also:

On the Standing Rock Reservation is found a yellow ocherous substance which, after being reduced to a fine powder, is used by the Indians in making yellow paint. This substance, when treated by means of heat, yields the vermilion used on all ceremonial articles as well as in painting the bodies of the Indians. The baking of this ocherous substance — a process which requires skill — is done by the women. First, the substance mixed with water is formed into a ball. A hole is dug in the ground in which a fire of oak bark is made. When the ground is baked, the coals are removed, the ball is placed in the hole, and a fire is built above it. This fire is maintained at a gentle, even heat for about an hour, which is sufficient for the amount of the substance usually prepared at a time. The action of the heat changes the color of the substance to red. When the ball is cold, it is pounded to powder. In the old days this red powder was mixed with buffalo fat in making the paint, but at the present time it is mixed with water. White, black, and blue paints were obtained by mixing colored earthy substances with buffalo fat. The blue was found in southern Minnesota (this required no treatment by heat), and the white and black in Dakota. It is said that white paint was preferred for the painting of horses because . . . other colors could be applied to advantage above it. Brown earth is (also) mentioned. . . .[6]

Clark Wissler listed the following colors used by the Blackfeet and their sources:

Yellow earth (as found)
Buffalo yellow (buffalo gall stones)
Red earth (burned yellow earth)
Red earth (as found)
Rock paint (a yellowish red)
Many-times-baked paint (a yellow earth made red by exposure to the sun)
Red-many-times-baked (a similar red, as found)
Seventh paint (a peculiar ghastly red-purple)
Blue (a dark blue mud)
White earth (as found)
Black (charcoal)[7]

Mallery listed trade colors employed on the Plains in 1880 as "vermilion, red lead, yellow chromate of lead, Prussian blue, chrome green, ivory black, lamp black, Chinese white, zinc oxide, all in the form of powder or in crude masses."[8]

Porcupine quills were the most commonly dyed objects. Occasionally feathers were dyed, especially red-dyed, but more often birds of suitable plumage colors were sought. The length of time the object was left in the dye pot determined the exact shade of color. Varying formulas, combining several dyestuffs, or mixing dyes with other substances (mordants) which helped to "develop" the color of an individual ingredient were also known. Interested readers can obtain an idea of similar formulas used by the Chippewas (Ojibwas) from a study by Frances Densmore.[9] The vessel used for dyeing also could influence the final color to some extent. Using the same dye solution, objects dyed in copper would be different in color from those dyed in iron, for example.

Early dyes used in coloring woolens traded with the Plains tribes were seldom color-fast. Often the cloth, on being boiled, furnished color for quill and feather dyeing. In more recent times, colored crepe paper was used as a source of dye in the same fashion. Needless to say, most Indian dyeing today is done with readily available aniline dyes.

To apply stains, the color-containing material was merely rubbed over the hide. The same effect can be obtained by applying, in small quantity, the proper shades of dry tempera (poster paint). Blackfoot costumes were often treated in this way to make them a dark ground color, which was almost as characteristic on the Plains as yellow-stained skins were typical of the Apaches in the American Southwest:

"Paints were ground to a powder in shallow stone mortars and mixed for application with . . . glue . . . obtained from boiling hide scrapings or the tail of a beaver."[10] In some instances, the color was simply mixed with water and the glue applied as an overcoating. Paints were stored in skin bags; many of these pouches are illustrated by Alfred Kroeber.[11] Brushes were made of the porous part of bison bones (spongy bone at knee joint or shoulder blade) or of chewed willow or cottonwood twigs. In painting, patterns were pressed into the hide with a flattened stick, and the paint was applied over areas so marked. Willow sticks of different lengths were sometimes used as rulers. Designs as illustrated in Figure 6 and Color Plate I were applied by the following tribes: A, border and box: Pawnees, Blackfeet, Mandans, Hidatsas, Crows, Cheyennes, Arapahoes, Utes, and the Western Sioux; B, border and hourglass: Kiowas, Comanches. Wallace and Hoebel suggest that the hourglass is the stylized symbol of the bison.[12] Feathered circle (see Color Plate 1): Western Sioux, Blackfeet, Hidatsas, Assiniboins, Arikaras; E, horizontal stripes: Blackfeet, Sarsis; F, bilaterally symmetrical: Western Sioux,

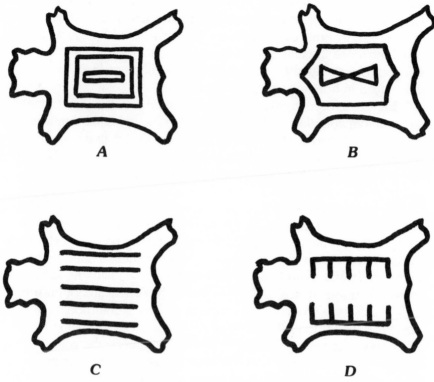

Figure 6. Painted-hide designs.

Cheyennes, Arapahoes. Bilaterally symmetrical here indicates two matching but separate units.

Designs on parfleches, quivers, and medicine cases are quite different from those on bison-hide robes; designs were somewhat related to the objects decorated. John Ewers has commented briefly on the development of representative art in Plains robes.[13] He noted improvement in artistic techniques over the years, and emphasized tribal and individual differences in representing horses and men. He made no mention of exploit marks—marks on hide shirts, robes, or leggings indicating valorous deeds. For example, among the Plains Crees, red paint on clothing marked a scar underneath. A long horizontal stripe on the robe signified a long war trip; a cross on a robe stood for engagement in a peace parley.

According to Mallery:

The following characters are marked upon robes and blankets, usually in red or blue colors, and often upon the boat paddles. Frequently an Indian has them painted upon his thighs, though this is generally resorted to only on festive occasions or for dancing [Figure 7]:

[A] denotes that the wearer sucessfully defended himself against the enemy by throwing up a ridge of earth or sand to protect the body. . . .

[B] signifies that the wearer has upon two different occasions defended himself by hiding his body within low earthworks. The character is merely a compound of two of the preceding marks placed together. . . .

[C] signifies that the one who carries this mark upon his blanket, leggings, boat paddle, or any other property, or upon his person, has distinguished himself by capturing a horse belonging to a hostile tribe. . . .

[D] signifies among the Hidatsa and Mandans that the wearer was the first person to strike a fallen enemy with a coup stick. It signifies among the Arikara simply that the wearer killed an enemy.

[E] represents among the Hidatsa and Mandans the second person to strike a fallen enemy. It represents among the Arikara the first person to strike the fallen enemy.

[F] denotes the third person to strike the enemy, according to the Hidatsa and Mandan; the second person to strike him according to the Arikara.

[G] shows among the Hidatsa and Mandan the fourth person to strike the fallen enemy. This is the highest and last number; the fifth person to risk the danger is considered brave for venturing so near the ground held by the enemy, but has no right to wear a mark therefor. The same mark among the Arikara represents the person to be the third to strike the enemy.

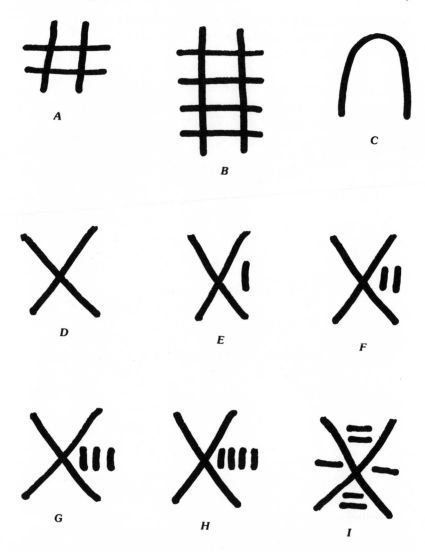

Figure 7. Characters used by some tribes. Adapted from Mallery, "Picture-Writing of the American Indians," Bureau of American Ethnology *Tenth Annual Report, 1888–1889* (1893).

[*H*] according to the Arikara, represents the fourth person to strike the enemy.

According to the Hidatsa, the wearer of mark [*I*] had figured in four encounters; in those recorded by the marks in each of the two lateral spaces he was the second to strike the fallen enemy, and the marks in the upper and lower spaces signify that he was the third person upon two other occasions.[14]

The Sioux painted a red hand on blankets or on bison robes to indicate being wounded by an enemy, while a black hand indicated the killing of an enemy.[15]

Indians painted their faces for decorative purposes and for protection against the wind, sun, snow and insects. Designs of various kinds were used to designate membership in certain societies, to prepare for ceremonies, to mark achievement, and to mourn for the dead. When used for personal ornamentation, there was no guide to the way it should be applied beyond the individual fancy of the wearer.

. . . [Paints] were mixed with fat before being applied. When painting for protection against the elements, the Indian rubbed grease made from buffaloback fat into his palms and then rubbed it in on his face. Then he would put his greasy fingers into his bag of powdered paint and rub that which adhered to them evenly all over his face. When the whole body was painted the fingernails were frequently drawn over the paint, producing a peculiar barred appearance.

Among the Omaha, a leader of a war party painted diagonal lines on his face from the bottom of the eyes to the neck. These represented the path of his tears while crying for the success of his expedition. Returning warriors who had taken scalps painted their faces black before entering their home village. Pawnee scouts painted their faces white to symbolize the wolf whose medicine was considered to be of the greatest help in scouting. Red paint was generally applied to the face of persons taking part in ceremonies or who were being initiated into

31

societies. Animal figures were sometimes drawn on the body to indicate the totem of the family to which the person belonged.[16]

Blackfoot single men painted stripes, circles, and/or dots on the face (seldom the body) with vermilion, yellow, white, and black paints. Face paints of red ocher, yellow ocher, white clay, white clay made pink with grape juice, and, for some dances, charcoal, were prepared by the Mandans. Osage men put red paint around the hair, the eye sockets, and the ears ("national colors"). Pawnee men painted their bodies with stripes of red and yellow, and the Otos usually painted both the body and the face, most frequently with red. Otos also covered their roaches with vermilion. The Pawnees took great pain to tip the eyelids with vermilion.

In the Sioux Sun Dance, ". . . the dancers were painted by the men whom they had selected for that purpose." A few of [Densmore's] informants stated that the bodies of the dancers were painted white on the first day of the ceremony, the colors being added on the morning of the second day, but others, including *Itun'kasanluta* (Red Weasel) stated positively that the painting in colors was done before the opening of the dance. Red Bird stated that each man who was accustomed to paint the dancers had a special color, which was "associated with his dream," and that "he used this color first in the painting."
The first warrior who killed an enemy had the right to wear the "black face paint"; thus many of the war songs contain the words "the black face paint I seek." This paint was worn by the man in the dances which followed his return from war. Usually it covered only the face, although a man might paint his entire body if he so desired. The second warrior to kill an enemy might "strike the enemy," for doing which he might, on his return, let his hair hang loose, but not paint his face. The time for continuing this practice varied according to the individual, but was usually about a month. If a war party defeated the enemy without loss to themselves, it was permitted to the first four who killed enemies, and also to their women relatives, to use the

Figure 8. Cheyenne Sun Dance sketches. Adapted from Cohoe, *A Cheyenne Sketchbook* (Norman, University of Oklahoma Press, 1964).

black face paint. In such an event special songs would be sung, and at any large gathering these four men would appear, the tribe considering them all to be equally entitled to the honor of using the black paint.[17]

Arapaho women painted streaks down their faces on cheeks, forehead, and nose, signifying war. Old women painted a spot on each cheek-bone and one on the forehead. A spot between the eyes signified a buffalo calf, and a line from the mouth down the chin represented a road. This whole painting signified peace.[18]

The Assiniboins had eyes surrounded by white clay; the rest of the face was red or reddish-brown (blackened to indicate an enemy had been killed). They tattooed two black stripes from the neck down the breast, applying charcoal into pricks made with a pointed bone.[19]

Tattooing was practiced among the Kansas and among the Caddoes.[20] Mandan men were tattooed on the right breast and right upper arm with black parallel lines and a few other figures; women were tattooed on the lower part of the face.[21] D. G. Mandelbaum pictures stripes on the arms and chests of Plains Cree men and stripes on the chin of Cree women, stating that tattooing was a common practice among Omaha women, a black circle tattooed on the forehead representing the sun and a four-pointed star on the chest representing night.[22] The Hidatsas often bore tattooing over half the chest. Indians of either sex could be tattooed among the Osages and the Crows. Crow women often had a circle tattooed on the forehead, a dot on the middle of the nose, and/or a line from the lips to the chin. Pricking was done with porcupine quills, and charcoal from red willow and from pine was rubbed in.

4. QUILLWORK

When talking of quillwork, one usually thinks of porcupine quills. However, as was pointed out earlier, the quills of birds, especially those of gulls, were occasionally used in some quilled objects, particularly to cover large areas. Bird quills, because of their pithy centers, took native dyes better than porcupine quills; early objects containing green—a difficult color to "take"—were, therefore, often of bird quills.

A careful study of objects containing brown "quillwork" often shows that the "quills" are, in reality, the stems of the maidenhair fern, which were used in the same places and in conjunction with actual quills. William Orchard, who made a definitive study of this art form, points out that

> four sizes of quills were found on the porcupine, and [these] were graded accordingly. The largest and coarsest came from the tail. . . . The next size came from the back, and still smaller quills from the neck. The finest were taken from the belly. . . . The various sizes were kept in separate receptacles made from a bladder of an elk or a buffalo.[1]

Porcupines existed in every area of the country where Indians produced any amount of quillwork. Little, if any, quillwork was executed in the southern Plains. Quilled objects included hair ornaments, shirts, leggings, moccasins, armbands, breastplates, and the

35

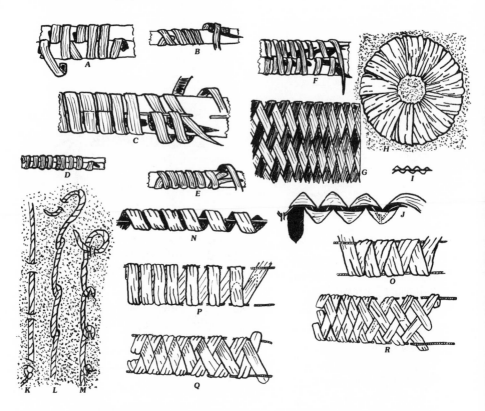

Figure 9. Quillwork. *A* to *F:* methods of wrapping with quills; *G:* plaiting; *H:* rosette formed by wrapping quills around an inner and an outer thread; *I:* quilled edge, shown in detail in *J; K:* spotstitch; *L:* backstitch; *M:* loopstitch; *N:* sewing quills with one thread; *O:* with two threads in diamond technique; *P:* two threads, one quill; *Q:* two quills; *R:* three quills. Dotted lines in *P* and *R* show the method of working in new quills. Adapted from Clark Wissler, "Material Culture of the Blackfoot Indians," American Museum of Natural History *Anthropological Papers,* Vol. V, 1910; William C. Orchard, "Technique of Porcupine Quill Decoration among the North American Indians," Museum of the American Indian *Contributions,* Vol. IV, 1916; and Carrie A. Lyford, *Quill and Beadwork of the Western Sioux* (Lawrence, Kansas, Bureau of Indian Affairs, 1940).

Figure 10. Tapered lanes in quillwork.

---

like. Tribal differences in techniques were rare, suggesting long-time use of quills in decorating clothing and other objects.[2]

Generally, after being dyed and sorted by size, the quills were flattened. Often, the quillworker used her mouth to hold several quills at the same time. This kept them soft and pliable; they were flattened by drawing them between the teeth as they were removed. Splicing of quills was done in two ways: (1) by a half-twist, the two ends being covered by subsequent quillwork; or (2) by covering one quill with the next, and the end being held in place by the first fold of the new quill.

Objects were often wrapped with quills, including the bases of scalp locks such as those seen on "war shirts," feather shafts, fringes (both of rawhide and of tanned leather), pipestems, etc. Soft objects such as hair were merely wrapped. Stiffer materials were wrapped using a sinew thread on the reverse side to hold the quill ends. For details of wrapping, see Figure 9, *A* to *F*.

To wrap objects such as pipe stems, the Western Sioux used plaited quillwork done with two quills, intertwined between two parallel sinew threads.[3] The finished product was similar to that produced by two-quill sewing, as illustrated in *Q*. Another form of plaiting is shown in *G*.

Sinew threads were used to hold down quilled bands. These could be applied with one of three stitches, illustrated in *K*, *L*, and *M*, depending on the object being quilled and, to a very minor extent, the tribal identification of the quillworker.

Various sewing techniques are shown in *N*, *O*, *P*, *Q*, and *R*. In early-sewn Western Sioux work, bands were always of the same width. Early Blackfoot work, by contrast, often contained bands which tapered at the ends. Western Sioux floral and realistic work, common about 1900, had tapered lanes (Figure 10). Strips of raw-

38

hide could be used as fillers in quilled bands to provide a firmer finished product and perhaps aid the worker to some extent.[4] Quilled rawhide strips were used by the Sioux to make breastplates, cuffs, arm bands, knee bands, bull-tail hair ornaments, and feather-shaft decorations—even hatbands and belts in modern times. Occasionally two flattened quills of different colors were used back to back in the one-quill-diamond technique (Figure 9, *O*), giving an esthetically pleasing color effect.

Rosettes were frequently made in quillwork. The circles on the dress in Figure 11 are nothing more than concentric circles of quilled bands. Rosettes could also be manufactured as shown in Figure 9*H*; the inside loop of sinew thread was drawn tight when the quilling was completed. Rosettes could also be made by closely stitching down lengths of wrapped hair to the object being decorated.[5]

Quills could also be used on the edges of garments; one technique used is shown in Figure 9 (*I*, as it appears; *J*, the detail of construction). Quilled edging was comparatively rare on the Plains, the distribution being peripheral and closely related to beaded-edging occurrence, to be described later. Other relationships to beadwork are in designs used and, according to some writers, techniques employed (one-thread sewing being done by the same tribes that later used overlay stitching in beadwork), although this doesn't always hold true. The Blackfeet, who used overlay stitch in beadwork, did little one-thread sewing in quills.

"Designs were laid out with the aid of cut patterns, sometimes made of rawhide or birchbark, or were drawn freehand (using a marker). . . . In this part of the work the women oftentimes were aided by suggestions from the men."[6]

Quill plaiting was a characteristic technique of the Mandans.[7] There are also many examples of plaiting on articles of the Sioux,

Figure 11. Facing page: *Pshan-Shaw,* the "Sweet-scented Grass," the twelve-year-old daughter of an Arikara chief. Painting by George Catlin, 1832. The dress, of mountain-sheep skin, is decorated with quilled rosettes; the robe of young bison hide has a quilled sunburst design. Courtesy of the Smithsonian Institution, Washington, D.C.

Poncas, Iowas, Cheyennes, Hidatsas, and other tribes.[8] The wrapping of horsehair with quills was commonest among the Crows and the Nez Percés. Quillwork was often used in combination with bead-work, even into the twentieth century. Quillwork is still being made by the Sioux, among others.

5. NATIVE ORNAMENTS

Perhaps one of the most complete studies of a single decorative object used by the Indians of the Plains was the study on hair pipes by Ewers.[1] His paper is especially outstanding because of its heavy dependence on pictures and archival records. Hair pipes are long tubular beads. First made by Indians from the columella (central column) of a conch, they were later manufactured by white settlers for trade with the Indians, being made of glass in the seventeenth century and of silver and brass in the eighteenth century (the metal ones were unpopular—they were probably too expensive). Hair pipes were manufactured from large shells in New Jersey in the later 1700's and arrived on the Plains in the early 1800's. The most popular early use was as hair ornaments; this use, first noted among northern tribes, spread as far as the Cheyennes, but by 1880 was obsolete.

Ear pendants of hair pipes were noted as early as 1806, especially among tribes whose men shaved a large portion of the scalp. The Kiowas used brass earrings, from each of which was suspended a hair pipe, which in turn supported a brass chain with a German-silver ornament at the end. Necklaces of hair pipes were observed by George Catlin among many Plains tribes in the mid-1800's; this usage was most popular among the Western Sioux, whose hair-pipe necklaces became more elaborate after 1890. This item was rarely worn by Blackfoot women.

Hair-pipe breastplates were probably invented by the Comanches around 1850. They had spread to the Western Sioux by

41

1870 and to the Assiniboins by 1880, becoming very popular with the introduction of bone hair pipes. Now they are also reproduced in plastic. Such breastplates are practically indispensable to many modern powwow dancers, including Crows, some Sioux, and some Southern Plains fancy dancers. There are three general breastplate styles: (1) two vertical rows of long hair pipes separated by a row of short; (2) three rows of long; (3) two rows of long separated by brass beads.

Commercially made and traded bone hair pipes (derived from bone stems of corncob pipes) arose in the early 1880's. Hair-pipe chokers arose among the Osages, the Otos, and southern tribes after this, but they were never very common. The Western Sioux and their neighbors preferred chokers of dentalium shells.

Bandoleers of hair pipes were observed among the Omahas and the Western Sioux after 1890. Such bandoleers are now used by straight dancers.

Texture, color, durability, appearance, and ease of handling as well as availability all had a share in determining the distribution and utilization of various native materials.

Hair and fur were commonly used in costuming. Scalp locks, or merely bundles of hair from the head of an enemy, were frequently used as decoration on the war shirt or on the leggings of a Plains warrior. Bison tails ("bull tails") were often decorated with quillwork or beadwork and used as hair ornaments. Hair from horses, deer, skunk tails, turkey beards, and from porcupines (the "guard" hair surrounding the quills) was used to make roach headdresses.

Ermine skins were popular in decorating costumes. Carl Bodmer pictured their use; John Ewers mentions their attachment to neck and sleeves of Blackfoot men's shirts. Lewis and Clark described a Shoshoni choker consisting of an otter back four or five inches wide to which was attached between one hundred and two hundred and fifty rolled ermine skins, in bundles of two or three; these were narrow ermine strips rolled around a grass core. The ermine rolls reached almost to the waist, forming a short "cloak."[2]

Other than bison hides, one of the most widely distributed and used furs was otter. It was frequently used in making medicine

42

pouches and, as we shall see, turbans. An otter-fur breast ornament was frequently a part of the "long John" Indian costume.[3]

Use of weasel (ermine), skunk, wolf, and fox skins was more common among northern Plains tribes and on the Plateau. Prince Maximilian mentioned that strips of skunk fur and wolf tails worn at the heels of a Mandan warrior signified war honors. Edward Curtis said that, among the Hidatsas, men who had counted coups wore foxtails in the same place. Lewis and Clark mentioned that the Sioux wore skunk skins attached to their heels and sometimes tucked them in the belt or carried them as a pouch. Although the practice was uncommon, skunk skins were also sometimes worn around the knees (the tail could be left intact). Blankets were woven from strips of rabbit fur by several Plateau tribes. Cohoe has even illustrated a headgear made from the stuffed pelt of a small rodent.[4] In the northern area, mittens were sometimes fashioned of animal fur. Among some tribes, fur strips were plaited into, or used to wrap, braids of hair.

Buffalo hair was made into wreaths and bands worn on the forehead and into necklaces. It was used to lengthen natural hair (although horse hair was superior for this purpose). Rudimentary blanket weaving may have been done. It was used as a stuffing material—for example, as winter fill for moccasins. Bunches of buffalo hair were used as paint brushes.[5]

The hard parts of native animals often were incorporated into the decoration of Plains costumes. The most commonly used objects of this nature were the claws of the grizzly bear. Feder and Chandler have prepared a very definitive work on necklaces made from these claws.[6] Natural yellow claws were the most highly prized. They were often strung on a cord by the Blackfeet, Crows, Gros Ventres, Western Sioux, and tribes of the Plateau. The Sioux often colored the undersides of the claws with vermilion. Dried human finger tips were unique spacers in bear claw necklaces among the Utes. Beads, brass bells, smaller claws—even fish vertebrae—have been used as spacers between claws in necklaces. Sometimes the Eastern Sioux made a necklace of the entire front bear paw, although this was uncommon. Among the Plains Crees and the Plains Chippewas, the claws were

44

strung on a piece of folded fur, skin, or cloth. The material was folded lengthwise, then little folds were made between each claw as it was strung. Claws could be fastened to the side of an otter skin, using the tail and the head of the otter as decorative ends; this was a common necklace among the Pawnees and, very probably, among the Mandans, the Hidatsas, and the Arikaras. Arikaras often decorated the head and tail ends with ermine strips. Finally, claws could be attached to an otter-fur choker. To this was attached a separate otter skin, tail hanging down the back, not too different from one type of otter turban to be described later. (The tail could be decorated.) This choker was common to the Prairie tribes.

Crows decorated grizzly-claw necklaces with circular pieces cut from bleached bison shoulder blades polished and smeared with white clay.[7] Claws of the eagle were also sometimes used in place of grizzly claws in making such a necklace.

One need only read the *Journals* of Lewis and Clark to see how common grizzly bears were in the nineteenth century. Since these animals have diminished in numbers, Indians have carved imitation bear claws from elk horns, cow horns, mountain-sheep horns, horse hooves, wood, and from celluloid harness rings.

Dewclaws (sometimes called "toes") and hooves were attached directly to clothing. Hidatsa women decorated the bottoms of their dresses with deer hooves if their husbands had counted coups. Cheyenne women decorated dress bottoms and sides with deer hooves. Arikara women wore hooves of mountain sheep at the shoulders. Mandans decorated with antelope and deer hooves. In

---

Figure 12. Facing page: *Blackfoot Medicine Man.* Painting by George Catlin, 1832. "Besides the skin of the yellow bear . . . are also the skins of snakes, and frogs, and bats, beaks and toes and tails of birds, hoofs of deer, goats, and antelopes; and, in fact, the 'odds and ends,' and fag ends, and tails, and tips of almost everything that swims, flies, or runs, in this part of the wide world." (George Catlin, *Letters and Notes . . .* , New York, Wiley and Putnam, 1841, I, 40.) The rattle and spear supposedly possessed supernatural power for healing and curing. Courtesy of the Smithsonian Institution.

45

more recent times dew claws were made into bandoleers; in the absence of dewclaws, thimbles, glass "chandelier beads," and other small objects have been used in making bandoleers.[8]

Deer and elk milk teeth, bear canines, rodent incisors, horse incisors, and bison teeth have all been mentioned by early observers as decorative devices, although the most highly valued were the permanent canine teeth of the elk. Crow women wore as many as eleven hundred elk teeth on one dress, although three hundred was the usual number. There is little evidence that men wore elk teeth, except in necklaces, together with bear claws and other pendants, or alone as good luck charms. Teeth were sometimes lightly incised with simple geometric designs. Distribution of elk teeth as decoration appears to be wide, at least on the northern Plains (central Plains in late historic times). The first users were probably the Mandans.[9] Elk teeth were so prized that imitations of them were sometimes carved from bone.

Roach spreaders were often carved from elk antlers. Bison horns were sometimes attached to feathered bonnets or used as part of special ceremonial headdresses. Horn sections were also sometimes fashioned into bracelets.

Mollusks obtained originally from the Pacific were traded with most Plains tribes. The most valued shells were dentalia, or tooth shells. Trade in these was noted as early as 1813. "The best quality are two inches long. One fathom (six feet) of these shells is valued at three blankets of two and a half points. . . ." White traders supplied shells from the Mediterranean and from the South Pacific also.[10]

Hair pipes did not become popular in Western Sioux chokers because dentalia were much preferred for this purpose. The author's wife owns a Western Sioux dress of blue strouding, the yoke of which

---

Figure 13. Facing page: *Chief of the Assiniboins.* Painting by Paul Kane, 1842. The chief has a small braided lock over the forehead and owl feathers in his hair and on his staff. He wears earrings and a grizzly-claw necklace; his shirt is decorated with bands of pony beads and wrapped fringes. There are many arrows in his wide quiver. Courtesy of the Public Archives of Canada.

is solidly covered with dentalia; this dress style seemed quite common among the Western Sioux, judging from 1890-to-1930 photographs, and will be mentioned again later. The Nez Percés even wore dentalia transversely through the nasal septum. Another popular Pacific mollusk shell used on costumes was that of abalone, which is lined with mother-of-pearl.

Cowries, and also Pacific mollusks, were fairly common, especially as attachments on dresses (similar to elk teeth in usage). Often, early writers wrote of jewelry of "shell," an all-encompassing word which makes a careful study of the kinds employed rather difficult. Lewis and Clark wrote of earrings made by Shoshonis from triangular pieces of shell and beads, and mentioned collars of sea shells. Rowena Thorp says that "ear ornaments were a mark of family, thrift, wealth, or distinction. Lakota, Cheyenne and other women wore long strings of shells hanging from the ear lobes, reaching to the waist." Earrings and necklaces of shell and bead were common among Kiowa women. Prettyman and Cunningham show seashell necklaces worn by Otos. Curtis says that the Arikaras favored ear pendants of large blue clamshells and mentions shell ear pendants worn by the Gros Ventres.[11] Trinkets of shell were probably used by most, if not all, Plains tribes. Silver conchas seen on later costumes were perhaps patterned after circular pieces of the Bahama conch shell (not clamshell pieces) often used in early costuming. A common Blackfoot choker was made of light blue necklace beads alternating with cowrie shells or, less commonly, with elk teeth.

Early beads fashioned from grass seeds, silverberries (*Elaeagnus argentea*), or dried rose hips were common before the advent of commercial beads. Red mescal buttons are strung today for neck-

---

Figure 14. Facing page: Gros Ventre group: Black Owl (left), Mary (standing) and an unidentified man (right). This is obviously a studio portrait. Black Owl has hair braids wrapped with fur and a hairpipe breastplate. Mary has elk teeth on her cloth dress. The man on the right wears a loop necklace. Each man has a single eagle plume in the hair and wears a striped blanket. Photograph taken around 1900 by David F. Barry. Courtesy of the Denver Public Library Western Collection.

laces and costume decoration. Necklaces of odorous roots were noted among the Blackfeet in the early 1800's and among the Mandans. A collar of quilled, twisted grass was observed by Lewis and Clark among the Shoshonis. Sage is used in making Sun dancers' headwreaths and wristlets. Cornhusks were "much used by the Cheyennes."[12]

Some large brown nuts were observed by the writer on the fringes of a Kiowa costume at the Field Museum of Natural History in Chicago. Other native materials sometimes used included St.-Cuthbert's-beads—single joints of fossil crinoid ("sea-lily") stems, thunderstones, snake skins, stuffed birds, and various minerals shaped into beads.[13] The Indian typically made use of any natural object that he came in contact with and liked, often incorporating these objects into his attire, either attached directly to clothing or worn as jewelry. Ear pendants were made from beads, shells, rings, wampum, and so on, and among some tribes it was not unusual to see over half a pound of jewelry suspended from each ear. Ears were often pierced, sometimes in many places, both at the top of the ear and at the lobe. Nose ornaments were also seen among some Plains tribes.

Objects of adornment sometimes had a symbolic meaning.

[One] . . . variety of symbolism that is found chiefly in connection with ceremonial objects attaches significance to various parts or appendages of such objects. For instance, feathers sometimes denote spirits, or again clouds, or wind, and hence breath and life. Fur, hooves, sticks, strings, bells, pendants, fringes, etc., are often symbolic in this way.[14]

Among the Plains Crees a single shaved stick worn in the hair indicated that the man had been wounded; two sticks, that a bullet had pierced his body. If his coat was slit into strips, he had held off the enemy singlehandedly. A man carrying a hooped staff with feathers had fought off the enemy, the number of feathers indicating their number.[15]

6. TRADE: BEADS

Trade between tribes occurred long before the arrival of Columbus. On the Plains, the Crows were noted as traders in traffic between the Upper Missouri River village people, especially the Mandans, and the Pacific coast. The spread of craft styles and techniques— floral designs in beadwork, for example—and of ceremonial ideas such as the Ghost Dance and the Peyote Cult resulted from communication and exchange between various Plains groups: "On the Plains and Prairies, trade consisted mostly of the exchange of products of the chase by the hunting tribes for the agricultural products of the farming tribes." Village tribes often obtained ceremonial garments in these exchanges. The Cheyennes held an important place in trade between tribes in the Plains culture area. Archaeological evidence indicates more and more that such exchanges have occurred for centuries over even more widespread areas in the Americas.[1]

Furs were the major commodity which the Indians had to offer— a commodity valued by Europeans to the present day. Beaver skins became the lingua franca of Indian trade, and goods were measured in "points," a point being worth one "made beaver"—a stretched and dried beaver pelt.[2]

The common denominator of Indian trade was the glass bead. The accepted definition of a bead is, "a little perforated ball of any suitable material intended to be strung with others and worn as an ornament."[3] In this section, glass beads only will be discussed; native

51

materials from which beads were fabricated have been mentioned previously. "Porcelain" in reference to beads came from descriptions of early shell beads by French explorers, who applied it to beads prepared from cowries (*Cypraea* shells).[4]

Shell beads (wampum) such as were common in the East were rare, if not completely absent, in the Plains area. Lewis and Clark, Catlin, and George Grinnell mentioned Indian manufacture of beads from fused sand—glass beads, if you will—but no examples have survived and the techniques described have serious flaws.[5] Glass beads were trade items carried by Christopher Columbus; popularly received then, their use as objects of exchange with the American natives never diminished. Beads, usually obtained from Italy, were traded by Europeans of all nationalities in the Americas—Spanish, French, English, Dutch. Beads found their way to the Plains from both the Atlantic and the Pacific. The Spaniards first introduced beads on the Pacific coast about 1770.[6] Highly prized at first, their value decreased as they became increasingly common.

Basically, beads were manufactured from colored capillary tubes. These were chopped up into minute particles in an iron gauge, using an iron instrument resembling a hatchet head. These cuttings were placed in an iron barrel containing sand and wood ashes and the barrel was revolved over a fire until the edges of the broken glass were rounded off. The finished beads were sifted into different sizes and hand-strung. Faceted beads were made either by rubbing the capillary tubes against an abrasive or by heating and faceting with a small metal spatula while the glass was molten. Other less common beads were made from a solid glass rod. The end of the rod was melted and a thread of liquid glass laid around a revolving iron bar. The diameter of the iron bar became the inside bead diameter. The center of bead distribution from colonial times onward was New York City.

The passage of time marked many changes in types of beads and their usage among American Indians.[7] Differences which must be considered include bead sizes and shapes, colors, beading techniques, designs used, and tribal preferences. The earliest beads introduced on the Plains were necklace beads. Not only were there plain-colored large beads (over one-fourth inch in diameter), called "Crow beads" or "China beads," but also the *Cornaline d'Aleppo*, a two-colored bead associated with mercantile trade of the town of Aleppo, Italy—first with opaque "Indian red" exterior and translucent dark green interior; later with opaque white interior and translucent, often red, exterior (known as an "underwhite"), often used in necklaces for children. On the northern Plains, these *Cornaline d'Aleppo* beads were also referred to as Hudson's Bay beads, as they were common in the early trade of the Hudson's Bay Company.

Polychrome necklace beads were sometimes traded with the Indians. An early polychrome bead, associated with trade in the East more than on the Plains, was the *Paternoster* (Our Father), or *Oldani*, bead, which had a chevron (also called a "star") pattern. Fancy, flowered beads were favored by the Crows and by many other tribes. Among the Blackfeet, a necklace of one type of bead—blue, with lines and flower buds in white and red—known as a "skunk" bead, was worth a horse and a robe. Brass beads, called "iron" beads by the Indians, were also an early trade item.

In the early nineteenth century, a smaller bead was introduced in trade. These were referred to as "real" beads, "pony" or "pony-train" beads because the traders traveled by pony, or "pound" beads because they were sold by the pound. Faceted or "cut" beads, known as "O.P." beads or "short bugles," seemed to appear in the 1840's. "Bugles," or "rods," were the longer beads of the beadmaker's sifter. "Seed" beads, much smaller than "real" beads, appeared in the 1850's; they were a product of Venice. A larger seed bead from Bohemia (Czechoslovakia) was introduced in the latter part of the century. It should be pointed out that "real" beads could be used side-by-side with quillwork, and seed beads and "real" beads were used at the same time by beadworkers in the same tribe.

Indians of North America used several techniques in working with beads. These included weaving, or "loom beading;" sewing— either for filling in areas or for putting on a decorative edge; netting; and stringing. Chandler and Kracinski have developed an outline (Table 1, page 55) which appears more workable than Orchard's although their "braided beadwork" perhaps should be grouped in a

general division with woven work, while sewn beadwork could probably be divided into "filling" and "edging."[8] This presentation will
deal with sewn beadwork and with the more common types of netting only; weaving was occasionally found only in the Prairie portion
of the Plains, and in modern costuming. In Figure 15, *A, B,* and *C*
indicate techniques for "filling." *D* illustrates what has been called
"triple-thread sewn" work; it might also be called "modified Crow."
Examples of this latter technique are rather rare, but it might have
been common in early beadwork; few early beaded items have been
collected.

Kracinski describes the use of the gourd-stitch technique to
make beaded strips, calling such use "strip netting."[9] Comanche
netting (*J*) uses threads as the "knots," where Peyote work (*I*) uses
beads as the "knots," or "loci." While Comanche netting is undoubtedly southern, it is now being done by the Sioux and Northern
Cheyennes.

The Blackfeet and their Plateau neighbors used both overlay
and lazy stitches, with more emphasis on the overlay stitch. The
Sioux and their neighbors, together with the Cheyennes and Arapahoes to the south, used lazy stitch almost exclusively. Beadwork
was equally divided between the two major methods among the
Assiniboins and the Gros Ventres. The Omahas and their neighbors,
the Poncas, the Osages, the Otos, and the Iowas, trimmed in overlay
stitch, while the Pawnees trimmed in lazy stitch. The Crows, Shoshonis, and Bannocks used the overlay stitch or the Crow stitch.

In wrapping an object with beads—for example, a calumet,
scalp lock, or ermine-tail attachment—the object was usually covered
with buckskin first; beads were sewn with the lazy stitch, about five
beads to a stitch. It is important to study the lane arrangement when
examining work created in the lazy stitch. This includes width of
lanes, flatness, matching of rows, and the position of rows in reference to the shape of the article. Lane width generally varied with
the object decorated.[10] Cheyenne work, as compared with that of
the Western Sioux, was quite flat, and rows were carefully matched.
There was a thriving exchange of beaded objects among tribes.

TABLE 1. BEADWORK TECHNIQUES

I. Woven Work
   A. Warp enclosed by weft
      1. Loose warp
      2. Secure warp
         a. Single needle weft
         b. Double needle weft
   B. Weft enclosed by warp
II. Sewn
   A. Single thread (lazy; edging)
   B. Double thread (overlay; Crow)
   C. Triple thread (modified Crow)
III. Braided
   A. Horizontal
   B. Vertical
IV. Netting
   A. Single thread
      1. Bead knot
         a. Open
         b. Closed (gourd, or Peyote)
      2. Thread knot
         a. Open
         b. Closed (Comanche)
   B. Multiple thread
      1. Bead knot
      2. Thread knot
V. Strung
   A. Single thread
      1. Knotted
      2. Unknotted
   B. Double thread

Source: Milford G. Chandler and David A. Kracinski, "Unusual Beadwork Techniques, Part I," *American Indian Tradition*, Vol. VIII, No. 5 (1962), 200. Material in parentheses provided by the author.

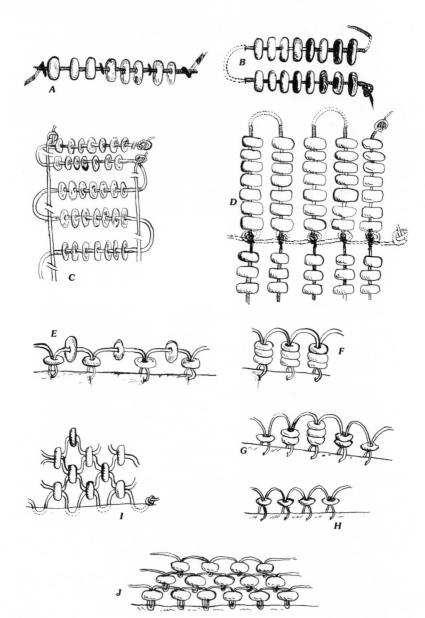

Sewn bead embroidery began with the advent of pony beads; these were usually fashioned into

extremely simple designs and appear to have been common to all the tribes in the (Plains) area. . . . On the Plains until about 1860 all beadwork looked very much alike. Knowledge of tribal distinctions which may have existed has now been lost.

Equilateral and isosceles triangles, usually pendant from a bar or stripe; sawtooth bands; bars and oblongs; and sets of concentric oblongs . . . [were] the elements used. [Early Western Sioux designs of this period were] almost all . . . groups of rectangles or lines broken up into rectangular areas.[11]

Among the Cheyennes, beaded stripes replaced bands once painted on clothing to represent war honors. More characteristic than the designs used was the loose floppy stitching and the larger beads.

With the arrival of seed beads (1850's), designs changed. The first designs fashioned from seed beads were very similar to designs created in pony beads; many were probably originally inspired by quillwork. Then several regional styles developed, as follows:

1. Blackfeet (and Plains Chippewas, Sarsis, Plains Crees, Flatheads, and Nez Percés). Figure 16: stripes were very common, and designs were not too different from older pony-bead designs. The mass effect of many beaded designs was a checkerboard effect, with C, the so-called mountain, often observed. Women's dresses in this area were frequently decorated with long, horizontal, parallel stripes stretching from left hand to right hand over the bodice and sleeves. The bands rise at the neckline, then dip to a V in front (see Color Plate 2).

2. Crows (and Hidatsas, Mandans, Arikaras, Shoshonis, and

Figure 15. Facing page: Beadwork techniques. *A:* overlay, or spot, stitch; *B:* lazy stitch; *C:* Crow stitch; *D:* modified Crow stitch; *E:* one-up, one-down edging; *F:* three-down edging; *G:* scalloped edging; *H:* one-down edging;

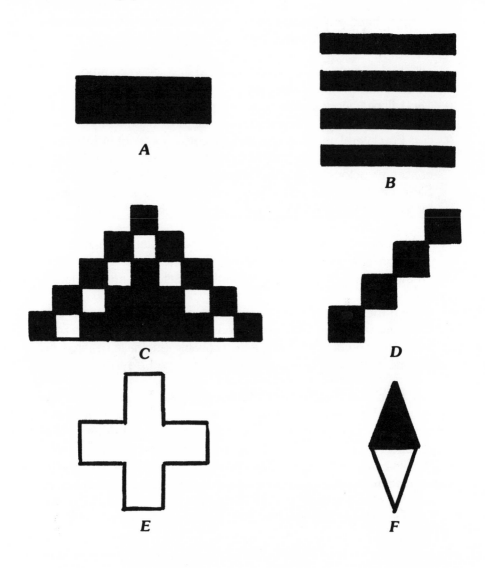

Figure 16. Blackfoot designs. *A:* stripe; *B:* series of parallel stripes; *C:* "mountain"; *D:* checker row; *E:* cross; *F:* "feather." Adapted from John C. Ewers, *Blackfeet Crafts* (Lawrence, Kansas, Bureau of Indian Affairs, 1945).

Bannocks). Figure 17: Triangles prevail, reminiscent of painted parfleche designs. This style appeared about 1880, later than the identifying styles of other tribal groupings.

3. Western Sioux (and Arapahoes, Cheyennes, Gros Ventres, Assiniboins, and Utes): the beadwork, which at first resembled Crow work (emphasis on triangles), began to emphasize narrow lines connecting design elements. Elements commonly used by Sioux women are shown in Figure 18; the names attached to the symbols here were given by particular beadworkers. They can not, and should not, be thought of as forming a symbolic code understood by all beadworkers of the tribe, and certainly not of the Plains area in general. White men's attempts to connect particular designs with particular meanings have always failed.

4. Comanches (and Kiowas and Kaskaias, or Kiowa Apaches): this beadwork emphasized beaded edgings and, later, very narrow beaded bands, no more than eight beads to a row. Designs used by the Comanches in these narrow bands appeared quite similar to Sioux designs, with special emphasis on small, wide-based triangles. An exception occurred in Kiowa cradles, which were often fully beaded with highly stylized semifloral designs thought to have been influenced by Delaware-Shawnee curvilinear designs (the Delawares and Shawnees were in contact with tribes of the southern Plains before "removal").

A late arrival on the scene, floral design was probably introduced by the Chippewas, Crees, and Eastern Sioux who, in turn, got the idea from European styles of the late 1700's. Older designs were done on black velvet without backgrounds; newer work, on white backgrounds. These designs spread to the Blackfeet and, from them, to the Crows, the tribes of the Plateau, and the Western Sioux. "Forced removal of many Great Lakes and eastern tribes to Oklahoma in the mid-1800's carried the floral style to the southeastern Plains."[12] The spread of floral designs occurred at about the same time as the development of realistic beaded designs in the Central Plains. Motifs such as men, horses, bison, elk, antelope, flags, swastikas, and so on, were now beaded onto items of apparel such as the

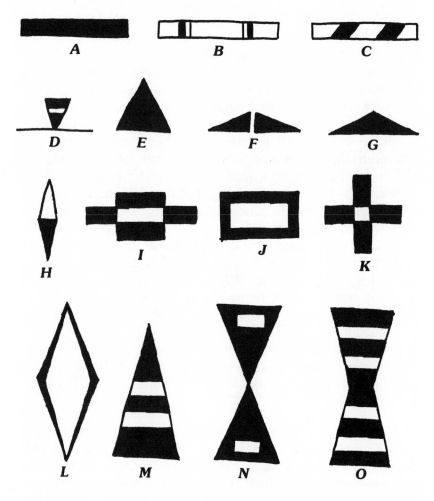

Figure 17. Crow designs. *A*: stripe; *B*: stripe divided by transverse stripes; *C*: stripe divided by diagonal stripes; *D*: isosceles triangle subdivided by narrow horizontal stripe; *E*: equilateral triangle, usually solid color; *F*: small right triangles, standing on broad base; *G*: isosceles triangle with wide angle, broad base; *H*: "feather" design; *I*: four rectangles surrounding rectangle of contrasting color; *J*: rectangle outlined in solid color, also called block;

newly introduced "vests." Such designs appeared among the Western Sioux about 1900.[13]

The Caddoes, like tribes on the east, made frequent use of velvet. Beaded edgings and the use of designs such as the "skydome" prevailed. Hexagons and a special type of triangle described as the "1890 triangle" are typical of Cheyenne work. A six-pointed star was a common design among the Iowas and the Otos. Arapaho work contains Maltese crosses, hexagons, and small solid squares. Common designs of Plains tribes are given in Table 2 (page 64).[14]

In very recent times woven beadwork has become somewhat popular on the Plains, especially with the white tourist. This popularity has been fed by importations from Hong Kong of inexpensive beadwork. The designs on these articles often do not resemble any designs used a few decades ago. Unfortunately many suppliers are now carrying these imported Chinese goods.

Particular color shades were apparently favored by certain tribes. In pony beads, blue and white were favorite colors, with some beadworkers using black, red, and amber. In the pony-bead period, the Blackfeet and Sioux seemed to prefer dark blue backgrounds, while the Arikaras, Mandans, and Hidatsas preferred white backgrounds. Real selectivity and tribal differences came with the advent of seed beads, however. In describing colors, several problems arise: (1) Differences in "lots" of supposedly the same color. Many a beadworker has encountered the problem of matching beads purchased at different times, even in Czech beads, which tended to be somewhat more uniform than Venetian beads. (2) Wide selection was possible. "Old bead sample cards used by traders prior to 1900 show more than eighty colors of seed beads from which Indian women could make selections." (3) Dating beaded objects is difficult, since "the tendency certainly exists to use beads over and over again. . . ."

K: blocky cross; *L:* diamond outlined with contrasting color; *M:* tall isosceles triangle elaborated internally either with smaller triangles or as illustrated, with horizontal bands; *N:* hourglass; *O:* hourglass, less constricted in center than *N.* Adapted from William Wildschut and John C. Ewers, "Crow Indian Beadwork," Museum of the American Indian *Contributions,* Vol. XVI (1959).

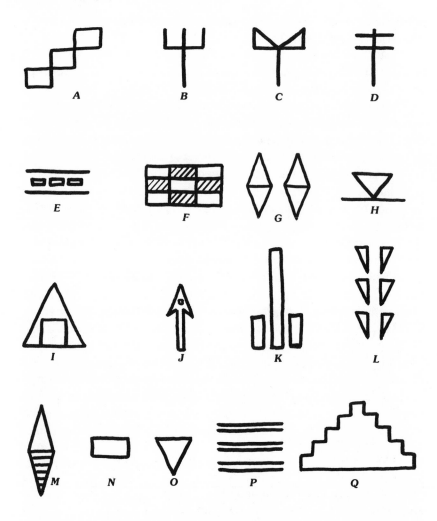

Figure 18. Western Sioux designs and names by which they were sometimes known. *A:* twisted; *B:* full-of-points; *C:* forked tree; *D:* dragonfly; *E:* filled up; *F:* tripe; *G:* feathers; *H:* leaf; *I:* tent; *J:* arrow; *K:* three-row; *L:* vertebrae; *M:* whirlwind; *N:* bag; *O:* pointed; *P:* trails; *Q:* cutout. The names varied among beadworkers. Adapted from Clark Wissler, *Indian Beadwork,* Guide Leaflet No. 50 (New York, American Museum of Natural History, 1931).

(4) Bead colors must be considered in combinations. (5) Powell's study, one of the best on the subject, described colors in terms of Ridgeway numbers; this requires conversion to bead color numbers, possibly resulting in some error.

Commonly used colors for several Plains tribes are given in Table 3 (page 65).[15]

Faceted seed beads were popular until 1870, especially among the Comanches. While their popularity has declined, they are still used. Certain bead sizes seemed to be used in some areas but not in others, perhaps because of availability, perhaps because of tribal preference. Powell's study gives no information on bead sizes; only in recent magazine articles have bead sizes been given.

> Small brassy or silver-faceted metallic beads . . . appeared on the Plains in the late Nineteenth Century. Considered in flat perspective, the "center of intensity" would be among the Dakota, followed by the Crow, Arapaho, and Cheyenne. In temporal perspective, metallic beads appear in the Eighties among the Dakota with some use by the Arapaho; they are abundant in the Nineties among the Dakota and infrequent among the Arapaho, Cheyenne, and Crow. The period of greatest Crow use of the beads appears to be around and after 1900. Metallic beads of this kind do not show up frequently on Blackfeet, Assiniboine, or Gros Ventre pieces. [Dakota here means Lakota, or Western Sioux.][16]

It should be pointed out that when beadwork is studied in relation to other decoration on an article of clothing more positive identification is possible. Weasel-skin tassels are *typical* among the Blackfeet; attached feathers ornaments, among the Crows and Sioux; horse or deer tails, among the Crows, Sioux, or Arapahoes; and tinklers, among Crows, Sioux, Arapahoes, and Gros Ventres. The key word here is "typical"; they were not exclusive. Tinklers (a metal device, discussed in the next chapter) can certainly be seen on articles of Kiowa, Comanche, Cheyenne, or Apache manufacture, for example.[17]

In addition to being used for embroidery on major articles of

63

TABLE 2. DESIGNS USED

T = Typical use F = Frequent use O = Occasional use	Utes and Shoshonis	Comanches	Crows	Blackfeet	Western Sioux	Arapahoes	Assiniboins	Gros Ventres	Cheyennes
Fork	T		O		T	T	F	F	
Feather		O	F	O	T		T	F	
Prong	F				F	F	F		
Diamond	O		T	F	F	T	O	O	
Diagonal checkers	O		T				O	O	O
Square		O	O	O	T	O	T	F	T
Twisted				T			O	F	
Square cross		O	F	O	T	F	T	O	F
Triangle	F	F	T	O	T	T	F	F	T
Stripe		O	O	T				F	T
Spreading	T					F	O	O	
Slanting bar	F	O	O			O			
Dragonfly					O			F	

TABLE 3. COLORS USED
(Combines all time periods)

	Kiowas and Comanches	Cheyennes	Arapahoes	Gros Ventres	Assiniboins	Western Sioux	Crows	Blackfeet
Light red	X	X	X	X	X	X	X	X
Rose underwhite	X	X	X	X	X	X	X	X
Oxblood			X			X	X	X
Orange			?				X	
Pale yellow				X	X	X	X	
Lemon yellow	X	X	X			X	X	X
Light green		X			X	X	X	X
Medium green			?	X		X		
Dark green	X		X	X	X	X	X	X
Light blue		X		X	X	X	X	X
Turquoise blue			?			X	X	X
Dark blue	X	X	X	X	X	X	X	X
Lilac pink	X		?	X	X	X	X	X
Chalk white	X	X	X	X	X	X	X	X
Black		X			X			X
Pearl white	X					X		

clothing, beads were fashioned into earrings (especially in the Prairie area), necklaces, and chokers. Chokers were

> two banded . . .; [each band] consists of a base of buckskin stuffed with some semisoft material. The two rolls measure 1 7/8 inches in diameter . . ., ornamented . . . with alternate bands of blue and white [pony] beads. . . . Strings of the same type of beads [are] pendant from the center of the front of this ornament. The choker was tied around the wearer's neck by two buckskin cords at the back. . . .[18]

A popular necklace among the Blackfeet and Crows was known as a loop necklace. This was made of either strung bone disks or of thongs wrapped with white beads. "The number of loops varies . . . 9 to 14 being the common range. Each loop is approximately ¼ to 1 inch longer than the one above." Loops were strung from "side-leathers" on each side. Pendant from a thong around the neck, side-leathers are about a foot long, slightly under ½ inch wide, and frequently decorated with brass studs. In the bone-disk type, "the center of each loop commonly has a single brass bead, although light blue cut beads and red underwhites are also common." In the bead-wrapped type, a short section of colored beads often was placed in the center portion.[19]

Assiniboins, Hidatsas, Nez Percés, Yakimas, Blackfeet, Gros Ventres, Sarsis, Sioux, and probably Crees also used this loop necklace. In addition to white beads, pink, light blue, and occasionally yellow beads were utilized.

Armbands were worn on gala occasions such as dances or ceremonies, and could be either beaded or quilled. They were about 2½ inches wide. Beaded pouches might serve as knife sheaths and awl cases or might hold paint, ration cards (in earlier times the same size and shape of pouch was used to carry flints and was known as a "strike-a-light" bag—it was usually about 4½ inches long and 2½ inches wide), toilet articles, sewing work, or a calumet. The calumet (pipe) bag was a soft bag one, two, or more feet long by about six inches wide, heavily fringed at the bottom; the basic size, shape, and length of fringe varied from tribe to tribe, as did the beaded decoration which it bore.

A very common belt pouch was about six inches square. The modern southern Plains woman's "belt kit" should be mentioned. It held an awl case and two bags and was sometimes constructed to be only ornamental, not functional.

Figure 19. Assiniboin dancers. Of particular note are the brass-stud belt, the ermine-trimmed otter necklace, and the striped shirt. Photograph by C. W. Mathers, Edmonton, Alberta. Courtesy of the Public Archives of Canada.

7. METAL

Objects of metal played an important part in the costuming of the Plains Indian, especially prior to 1880, at which time they seemed to lose their popularity. The type of metal made little difference.[1] Silver or gold were no more valued than metals considered of lesser worth by the European. Even pieces of brass kettles were valued and worn as decorative devices. Lewis and Clark noted among the Shoshonis the wearing of peace medals; iron and brass armbands and hair plates; bracelets of copper, iron, tin, and brass; pewter buttons; ornaments of sheet copper and brass and of brass wire. Bracelets of brass and copper were noted among the Nez Percés, as well as dress decorations of little pieces of brass (kettles?); brass rings were noted among the Cheyennes.

Trade or "give-away" items carried by Lewis and Clark included wampum; beads; ready-made shirts; bright kerchiefs and hankies; needles, thimbles, and thread; vermilion; axes, tomahawks, and knives; saddler's seat awls; ribbon and cloth; brilliant worsted "fairet" (quartering); sheet copper, tin, and iron; rings (described as "cheap, ornamented with colored glass or mockstone"); finger-size curtain rings; iron and brass combs; blankets; and silver arm and wrist bands, earrings, nose trinkets, "drops," broaches, and small medals. The expedition found that the most highly prized items were blue beads (first in demand), brass buttons (number two), knives, axes, toma-hawks, saddler's seat awls (for moccasin making), glover's needles,

69

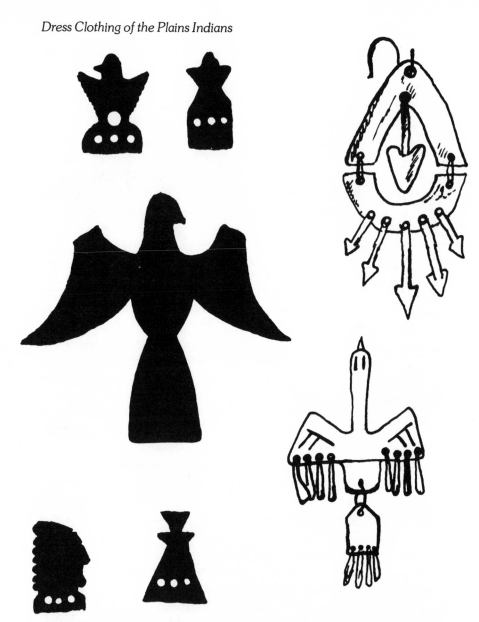

Figure 20. Metalworking in "Peyote style." Solid figures are diagrams of patterns used by metalworkers. Adapted from Norman Feder, "Plains Indian Metalworking," *American Indian Tradition*, Vol. VIII (1962).

iron combs, brass camp kettles (in "nests"), and metal arrow points.[2] Metal objects were less common in early trade at Fort Union (Assiniboins, Plains Crees, Plains Chippewas, Crows, and Blackfeet) than in trade with the Arikaras, Mandans, Poncas, and Teton Sioux.

One must not gain the impression that Indian trading began with Lewis and Clark, nor that a tribe had to deal directly with traders to have objects or materials from whites. As mentioned earlier, active trading occurred between tribes.

Brass wire was perhaps one of the earliest trade items. Ready-made brass objects in trade included bells, buttons, rings, armbands, large necklace beads, and hair plates. Brass tacks, or studs, became quite common on certain objects worn by the Indian. (Figure 19)

Silver objects were relatively rare on the Plains in the early nineteenth century. The commonest items were hair plates, which might be fashioned from silver dollars. They could also be obtained ready-made from traders; they had been traded at a much earlier date with Eastern Woodlands tribes. In addition to hair plates, silver was fashioned into pectorals, bracelets, and earbobs, and occasionally into bands for throat or forehead decoration. The Kiowas and the Comanches probably obtained silver ornaments (buttons, rings, and bracelets) in trade from Mexico.

German silver, which really contains no silver, but is an alloy of nickel, zinc, and copper, "was first manufactured in the United States by J. Wharton of Philadelphia in 1863."[3] For twenty years or so it was very popular among the Cheyennes and other southern tribes and still is often used.

"Plains Indians never learned to melt and mold metals; their major techniques involved pounding, cutting, and filing."[4] These methods were used, in order, when sheet metal (any kind) and files were available. Files were known, but scarce, at the time of the Lewis and Clark expedition. Little is done differently in the production of modern Peyote jewelry. (Figure 20) Using sheet metal, the basic design is cut with a crude, improvised chisel; the work is smoothed down with a file and finished and polished with emery cloth. An awl is used for punching any necessary small holes. Peyote jewelry includes bolo tie and kerchief slides, pins, and earrings. Other items

Figure 21. Bells used by Plains tribes.

made in the same style by metalworkers (not ritually used) include belt conchas, armbands, broaches, and roach spreaders.

Bells were traded with Eastern tribes by Jacques Cartier in 1535; they certainly were some of the first objects of trade on the Plains. According to Dennis Lessard, hawk bells

> came in various sizes and shapes. I have seen both oval and round, but the oval seems to be the preferred type and the most commonly used. They were of two piece stamped brass. Some very early ones were of spun (?) brass and, I think, hand-fashioned. These were very flat in appearance. From about the 1860's on, I'd say that hawk bells were popular in in the entire Plains area. [Figure 21][5]

Sleigh bells, sheep bells, and so on, also were commonly used in Plains costuming. According to Gallagher and Powell:

> Tinklers, small tin cone-shaped ornamental devices . . . appear on most kinds of garments, pipe-bags, and pouches. These tinklers appear on [Powell's] oldest Sioux specimens (1856 and 1860), are frequent in the Seventies, and over 40% of Sioux specimens of the Eighties show the presence of tinklers. Their use in the Nineties declines to about 30% and to about 15% in the decade 1900–1910. Tinklers appear on scattered pieces from other Plains tribes with the Crow showing a 25 to 30% frequency in the 1900–1910 period—double that of the Western Sioux for the same period. Again, as with . . . metallic beads, there is no indication that these small tinklers were com-

monly used by the Blackfeet, Assiniboins, and other northern tribes.[6]

Silver dollars were often pounded and worked into other objects. Large presentation coins, known as peace medals, were given to Indians in the East as early as 1670. While there are several major groups of these, we need consider only United States presidential-struck and fur-traders privately struck medals. The presidential medals have again been "issued recently by the mint and are sold as souvenirs. . . . While sharp, hard, and decidedly new," they are inexpensive, and easily ordered from a price list issued by the United States Mint in Philadelphia. These coins generally are and were three inches in diameter. "Presidential medals were made originally for presentation to American Indian chiefs and warriors. The Spanish, the French, and the British had presented medals to the Indians. To the Indians, they were tokens of government friendship, badges of power, and trophies of renown." Fur-trade companies struck medals to aid in their trading ventures; Indians who encouraged trade were recognized using these devices.[7]

Other coins, especially pennies, were used as decorative attachments. The author has a woman's breastplate—probably Western Sioux—the bottom of which has German pfennigs as decorations. Coins of many nations were used. "Brass ornamental coins are made and sold for trim only and come with the hole already in them. They . . . can be purchased in most trim shops."[8]

Cartier gave tin buttons as presents in 1535, indicating an early history for these devices:

Buttons of all types, flat, ball, convex, made of brass, silver, pewter, glass, pearl, bone, horn, German silver, cut steel, tin, iron, etc., were not used so much as garment fasteners as [they were used for] ornaments for parts of clothing. . . . The "shell button" . . . was composed of two parts. The face was a thin sheet or shell of silver, gold, brass (the latter being plain, silvered or gilt), which was, in turn, cemented to a base of wood, bone or cardboard. . . . [The] early method of gilding was done by placing gold upon the base metal buttons, mixed with mercury, and the latter then driven off by heat, leaving a thin layer of gilt (gold amalgam) on the button, after which it was burnished. . . . By 1819, five grains of gold, worth one shilling, were sufficient to gild 144 buttons of one inch diameter.

. . . The great button companies of New England (with few exceptions) did not begin active operations until around 1800. . . . By studying changes in . . . firm names (as stamped on the buttons) . . . dating of certain buttons becomes fairly certain. . . .

. . . When (military) uniforms changed and styles became obsolete, the . . . garments were . . . passed on to the Indians. . . .

The most popular type of brass button, which was distributed far and wide among the plains . . . Indians was the thin, flat brass button, in varying sizes from the large coat buttons to the small sleeve and waist coat fasteners. When issued, these were usually gilt and presented a very flashy appearance.

The earliest brass buttons were cast in one piece and the shank was a conical or wedge-shaped protuberance on the back. Later, a wire loop was brazed on the back and, until about 1860, the practice of buying the shanks from separate manufacturers and attaching them to the backs of the button blanks continued. Wire shanks were applied individually to these buttons with blow pipe and flux until around 1850. . . . Since these early shanks made of wire were hand drawn, they were not perfectly round, but tended to be oval in cross section [Figure 22].[9]

In spite of the reference in the Lewis and Clark trade lists to gaudy jeweled rings, most trade rings were plain bands, like modern wedding rings, of brass, copper, or silver (in that order).

Bracelets and armbands were made from quilled hide before the introduction of metals. One popular type of metal bracelet was a wide band of corrugated brass, which can be observed in many early photographs. Another common type was a one-inch-wide plain band of brass, iron, tin, or (rarely) silver, occasionally decorated with a scratched design. These bands were sometimes joined at the ends, but, more frequently, had holes on each end; thongs were laced

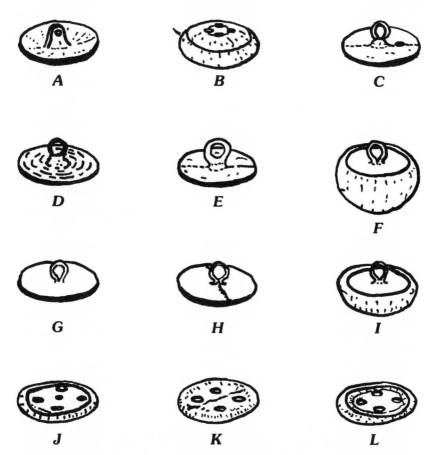

Figure 22. A variety of buttons. *A*: roughcast brass or bronze, with a hole drilled in the shank, 1700–65; *B*: bone or wood back and silver front, with holes for gut fastening, 1700–90; *C*: cast white metal (note the mold seam and slightly raised plug), with an iron-wire eye, 1760–90; *D*: cast white metal or brass, with a spun back and brass-wire eye (note the burr edge on the shank), 1760–85; *E*: cast white metal, the eye and button in one piece, 1750–1812; *F*: two-piece, pressed brass, with a brass eye soldered to the back, 1812–30; *G*: brass or bronze, with brass eye soldered on (eye has no foot), 1785–1800; *H*: similar to *G*, but the eye has a foot, and a restrike anvil seam is apparent, 1812–20; *I*: two-piece, pressed brass, with brass eye soldered to back, 1830 to present; *J*: bone (center hole to index turning tool), 1750–1830; *K*: one-piece, cast white metal, 1800–60; *L*: two-piece, pressed steel, post-1870. Adapted from Stanley J. Olsen, "Dating Early Plains Buttons by Their Form," *American Antiquity*, Vol. XXVIII (1963).

through these holes to keep the band firmly in place. In addition, bracelets were made by the Blackfeet from two pieces of heavy brass or copper wire twisted together and bent into a wrist band. The same materials were used in producing bands worn around the upper arm. German silver was used after its introduction.

Metal ear decorations were occasionally worn. The most popular type was an ear "wheel," a small silver concha. Superficially it resembled a small hair plate, but often bore an elaborate punched design. Metal ear "bobs," or drops, were also mentioned as early trade items; this type included the so-called "ball and cone" earrings (Figure 23). A large cluster (or clusters, when ears had multiple piercings) of earrings was often worn on each ear. Nose trinkets have been mentioned in the literature as trade items, but they were not commonly worn on the Plains.

Hair plates might be described as metal broaches worn attached to the hair, usually in graduated sets, the largest at the top and the smallest at the bottom. They were probably introduced from the Eastern Indian trade (Hudson's Bay Company and the Northwest Company) through the villages of the Upper Missouri (Mandan and Hidatsa). Their spread was undoubtedly influenced

> by the custom of wearing the hair long and decorating the long hair queue; by the intrinsic value of metal as a rare material; by the fact that previous knowledge of working metals was available; and perhaps, also, by an aboriginal copper industry.
>
> The use of hair plates apparently developed on the Northern Plains [around 1800] and then jumped to the South Plains [around 1820] before being introduced in the Central Plains area [around 1830]. . . . By the 1850's hair plates as an ornament were fairly common throughout the entire Plains area; however, metal ornaments were always comparatively rare because of the scarcity of white metals.
>
> Nickel silver was introduced into the Plains trade during the middle 1860's and immediately caused a tremendous florescence of metal-working. . . . Because metal ornaments were

fairly common after 1865, they lost their prestige value and soon dropped out of favor. Few Indians were wearing the larger metal ornaments after 1880, but limited quantities have continued in use to the present day.[10]

Superficial observation does not reveal any technical difference between hair plates and metal conchas. Conchas were placed on clothing (*see* Color Plate 3) and fashioned into belts.

"The concha belt seems to be a Plains invention (around 1865) as there is no prototype for it anywhere else. About 1870, the Navajo started to make their famous concha belts and Arthur Woodward believes that they obtained the idea from the Plains Indians."[11] "Droppers" seen on these belts were probably developed from a silver article on a horse's headstall.

Figure 23.
"Ball and
cone" earring.

Early belts were of stiff skin or rawhide, but commercial leather has been the standard belt material since the late 1800's. One common type of belt was the "tack belt," a strip of leather (among Blackfoot women, usually four inches wide) decorated with patterns in smooth-headed brass tacks. The tacks were pushed through the leather, the protruding shanks were cut off short, and the ends bent over. Most belts tied in the front, with a thong connecting one pair of holes. Among the Blackfeet, men's belts were very narrow.[12] Tack belts are no longer in style; it is not known when they lost popularity.

Pectorals, pendant objects worn generally over the chest region, were early gifts to Indians of both the East and the West. In the East, one of the most commonly depicted objects was a wide crescent or series of three crescents worn one under the other, often termed "gorgets." These crescents do not appear in early lists of objects given or traded on the Plains (Figure 24, *A*).

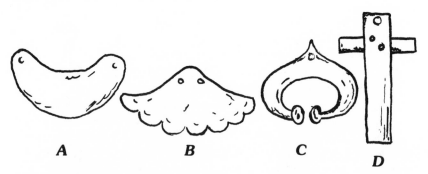

Figure 24. Metal ornaments. *A*: crescent; *B*: "cloud"; *C*: *naja*, *D*: cross.

The "cloud-shaped" pectoral (Figure 24, *B*) might have been derived from the central portion of a Spanish horse bridle. It usually bore scratched designs on one or both sides. The *naja* (*C*) is typically Spanish and is, to this day, a popular motif among the Navajos. The cross (*D*), when first introduced on the Plains, had *naja* ornaments attached and, therefore, undoubtedly was introduced through trade with the Spanish. Use of the cross on the Plains had no symbolism—Christian or otherwise—to the Indian; it was merely an attractive ornament. The side arm was frequently attached to the upright with rivets. The cloud and cross were produced by Indians from flat metal (German silver) and were common in the period from the mid-1860's to about 1880.

Certainly, as other metal items were observed by the Indians among whites, they might be sought as objects for trade. Rifle shells were used on Plateau breechcloths, for example.[13] One occasionally observes the use of metal chain in old photographs, especially in the fashioning of ear ornaments. Proof of existence of any small metal object in the Plains area for an extensive period of time probably proves its use, at least occasionally, on Indian wearing apparel.

Mirrors (looking glasses) were highly valued by Indians. Early mirrors were probably produced in Leipzig. Because they were fragile, Indians frequently mounted them in wooden frames, which might be painted, incised with lines or designs, or decorated with brass studs, feather dangles, or other decoration. Such mirror

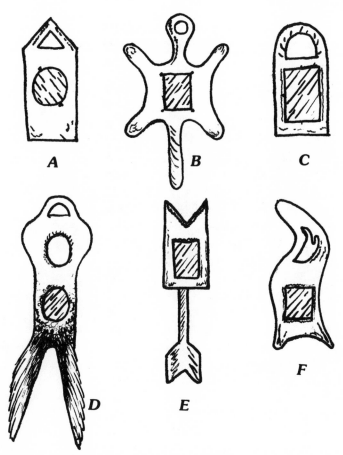

Figure 25. Mirror boards. *A:* Arapaho; *B:* Crow; *C:* Osage; *D:* Arapaho; *E:* Blackfoot; *F:* Pawnee.

boards are still popular as part of northern Plains costumes (Figure 25).

Sequins, rhinestones, and other costume jewels were added to apparel as they were introduced. Sequins (older sequins were of metal) were frequently attached to breechcloths and other clothing. Metallic fringe also was applied to garments as it was introduced. This fringe is used by some straight dancers on their clothing. Fringed uniform epaulets were also worn frequently on 'dress" clothing.

Figure 26.   Sioux Ghost Dance, at Pine Ridge, South Dakota. There was a decided shift to cloth from skins in the decade or so before this painting was executed in 1890. Often only moccasins were still made from skins. Painting by Frederic Remington, from the Library of Congress Collections.

8. CLOTH

Woolens were an early item traded with the North American Indians. Heavyweight woolen cloth was mentioned in early descriptions of trade in the eastern part of the country, where it quickly replaced winter garments of skins and furs, as it did when introduced on the Plains. One has a distinct feeling that the earliest trade was in better-quality beaver cloths, such as kersey (a lightweight beaver cloth made in Kersey, England), gloucester (Gloucester, England), and duffel (a heavyweight kersey from Duffel, Belgium). By the time of Lewis and Clark, the woolens traded in America were primarily made in Stroudwater, Gloucestershire, England, exclusively for American Indian consumption. This coarse "strouding," as it was called, usually was dyed scarlet red or dark navy blue (close to black). The woven cloth was dyed, rather than the yarn. Old blankets and other articles made from strouding have undyed selvages. If one looks at the peak of each triangular-shaped indentation of the selvage of white-edged cloth, he will see a hole left from the heavy thread which was used to sew a cloth (usually canvas) binding along the edge, which in turn was clamped to the dying machine to permit the strouding, a "trade cloth," to act as a blotter and soak up the excess dye from higher-quality material being dyed. Its being merely a blotter cloth explains its coarseness, the irregularity of the undyed selvage (the dye often running into the selvage), and the frequent spots that were not dyed all the way through—the middle of a cross section being left whitish.[1] Cohoe shows a wrap-around blanket in which pieces of red and blue

81

strouding have been attached along the white selvage edges.[2] It might be repeated that early dyeing was far from colorfast, and early strouding often served as a source of dye for coloring porcupine quills, and so on.

Lightweight woolen broadcloth (smoother than strouding) and flannels are mentioned in relation to Plains Indian gifts and trade items, but do not seem quite as popular. Ewers mentions "checkered, striped, and plaid materials," presumably flannels, given in the yearly annuities to the Piegans in 1858.[3]

Talk to any Indian in Oklahoma about broadcloth nowadays and you will find that he is talking about the rainbow-selvage styles (there are several) with a multicolored border. Any piece of good prairie ribbonwork is most likely colored-edge broadcloth (see Color Plate 4). The various types of broadcloth can be vaguely dated by the different types of edge.[4]

In addition to strouding yard goods, blankets were early trade items. "White, tan, red or green blankets with a dark stripe at each end were most common in the old days. Another favorite was the Hudson's Bay candy-stripe, a white blanket with four colored stripes at each end."[5] Wildschut and Ewers illustrate a pair of leggings made from a blue blanket with black stripes, the stripes across, and at the top of, the leggings.[6] Early blankets were also frequently marked with short parallel lines indicating their "point" value in trade for beaver pelts. "Mackinaw" blankets were heavy blankets which derived their name from Fort Mackinac, where great quantities were distributed. Blankets were often decorated with a beaded or quilled strip attached down the center from end to end. The beading here was usually done on a leather backing and the backed beadwork sewn to the blanket rather than beading directly on the less durable blanket itself.

On the northern Plains, and among Plateau tribes, a long hooded coat known as a "capote" was made from blanketing (Figure 27). Such a coat was sometimes decorated with cloth "epaulets" of a contrasting color and trimmed with beading or with other decoration.[7] Among southern Plains tribes, self-fringed Navajo blankets were common.

Of all items of apparel, the breechcloth (or breechclout) is one of the least common in museum collections, poorly illustrated both in early paintings and old photographs, and infrequently mentioned in the literature. Early Plains dwellers probably wore some type of protection on the lower trunk, either a breechcloth or an apron (a rectangle of material hanging from the waist).[8] Early breechcloths were probably of skin. While the breechcloth was usually a foot to a foot and a half wide, the length varied according to how the article was worn and by whom. It could be long in front, long in back, long on both ends, or short on both ends (with belt loops). Some were so long they dragged on the ground. Occasionally it was worn with a twist between the legs in the crotch area; this is the method of wearing the breechcloth in modern straight-dance costuming. Often it was made from 52- or 54-inch-wide strouding, with the white selvage at each end. This produced a covering which, when worn equally long in front and back, barely covered the buttocks with the rear flap.

Among the Crows, the preferred style was long in front. Sometimes, both decorated ends were worn in the front. Prettyman photographed a Pawnee breechcloth that was long in front. Wissler described a 12-by-54-inch Blackfoot breechcloth worn the same length in front and back. Cohoe drew short breechcloths on Osages; breechcloths long in front and back on Cheyennes. Generally, northern Plains breechcloths tended to be longer; central Plains, narrower and shorter, going only to the knee or halfway down the calf in front, slightly shorter in the rear.[9]

Breechcloths were decorated with ribbons, metallic fringe, sequins, tinklers, or other small decorations. Quilled or beaded breechcloths were rare if not nonexistent. Ribbon was often applied in horizontal lines in the front and in chevron pattern in the back.[10] Fringed plaid shawls were also sometimes used as breechcloths.

Perhaps a little more should be said about belts. Richard Conn described two types of Blackfoot women's belts and mentioned a third: (1) Belts decorated with brass tacks only—so called "tack belts." "Most tack belts tie in front with a thong connecting one pair of holes. Some . . . fastened with harness buckles, and a few even had two buckles like a motorcycle belt." (2) Panel belts, decorated

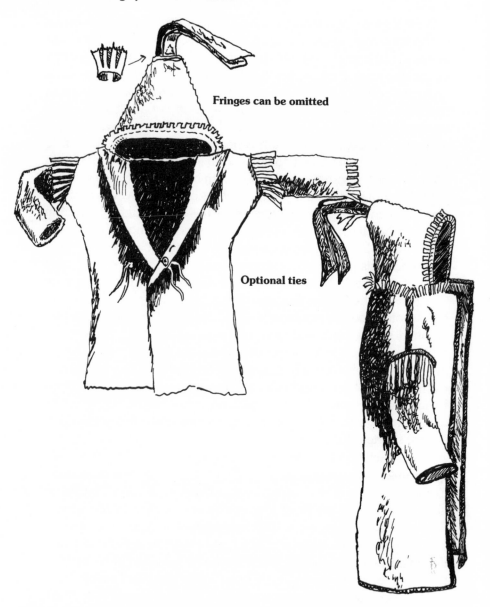

Fringes can be omitted

Optional ties

Figure 27. Construction of a blanket capote. Adapted from Bill Holm, "Making a Blanket 'Capote'," *American Indian Hobbyist,* Vol. III (1956).

with beads or with beads and tacks. The beaded panels were of long, loose, lazy-stitch bead rows, edged by single vertical rows of overlay beading. When the belt was worn, the beadwork tightened up. (3) Conn mentioned fully beaded belts, implying that they might have been more common among Blackfoot men than among the women. Fully beaded belts have wider distribution than among the Blackfeet only.[11]

Cloth patches or swatches were sometimes attached as ornamentation on early clothing. Wissler, for example, describes the following ornamentation on a Blackfoot dress:

> . . . double pendant thongs are placed across the skirt at intervals in two or three rows. Sometimes these are anchored to bits of red and black [navy blue?] cloth, encircled by beads. . . . Still lower, appears a triangular piece, half black and half red, and two rectangular pieces similarly divided. Duplicates of these appear again in the back [Figure 28].[12] Rectangular and triangular patches are shown in Figure 28, with two different methods of thong attachment. The beaded borders were very narrow, done with small beads in lazy stitch.

Even before Lewis and Clark, garments, usually produced in New York, were given as gifts to Indians and used in trade. Scarlet coats were well received. Army uniforms, with their fringed epaulets,

Figure 28. Thongs holding cloth patches.

Figure 29. · Blackfoot hat.

gilt buttons, and striped trousers often made their way into Indian hands. Knickers became popular among some tribes as they were introduced by whites, probably in the late 1800's. Vests were introduced about 1875 and were widely adopted among the Sioux. Hats became a common addition to the costuming of some tribes; a ten-gallon hat for a time was almost a trademark for the Blackfeet, both men and women (Figure 29).

Finger-woven sashes were sometimes obtained in trade, either from Indians to the east who made them (Prairies and Lakes area) or from the Hudson's Bay Company. The latter were usually wider, always longer, mass-produced "Assumption" sashes made by several villages of French Canadians near the city of Montreal. Often these Assumption sashes were in the flame pattern, but occasionally also in the center-reverse chevron. In producing the center-reverse chev-

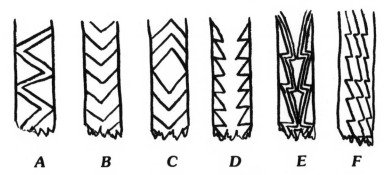

Figure 30. Assumption-sash patterns. *A:* zigzag; *B:* chevron; *C:* center-reverse chevron; *D:* arrow; *E:* flame; *F:* lightning.

ron pattern, the sash was actually turned around when half-braided (Figure 30).[13]

Originally, all cottons were referred to as calicoes, after a place in India. A printed calico, known to the Indians of North America as a "printed cloth," was also referred to as a chint (plural, chintz). Printed calicoes in the 1800's were a popular fabric item in Indian trade.[14] Calico printing of repeated small unit designs was an industry in its own right, particularly in France. One can see, in observing the Indian costumes of the Plains, changes which had occurred in white men's clothing styles not too long before; white shirts, close-fitting colored cottons, pin stripes—all had their day.

Other cloth items given or traded to the Indians included a variety of shawls (rumals, romals, rammals; sannis, cassas, demeties); kerchiefs and hankies; gartering (knitted fabric); headbands (garters and headbands were observed among the Mandans in 1738); and a variety of ribbon (riband).[15] Ribbons were attached as streamers to clothing and headdresses, used to edge the neck opening on some dresses and shirts, and applied on surfaces, such as on breechcloths, as previously noted. Ribbon appliqué, while primarily associated with more eastern tribes, was noted among the Iowas, Osages, and, to some extent, the Omahas, Poncas, Pawnees, Otos, and Kansas. In order of frequency, red, white, yellow, blue, and dark blue ribbons were used in older appliqué; newer aniline dyes brought green, pink, black, gray, tan, purple, and maroon.[16]

9. HAIR AND HEADGEAR

"The love of the heavy long tresses was a typical trait of the Plains."[1] Thus Wissler generalized about Plains hair styling, which varied by tribe, by sex, by age, as well as with time. Among some tribes, long hair was cut when loved ones were being mourned.

Nez Percé, and later Western Sioux, Crow, and perhaps Arapaho, men had an interesting upswept hairdo, or "pompadour," in front. Sioux men did this by frequent wetting, while the Crows used a heated stick as a curling iron.[2] This pompadour became so popular among the Crows that it was used in sign language to represent the tribe. With this hairdo the hair was worn long in back. Frequently, additional human hair (from Indians in mourning) was added to this rear mass to extend it to great lengths; buffalo hair and horsehair were used for the same purpose.

Scalp locks were small bunches of hair growing from the center of the scalp and often braided. Such locks were very common for men of many tribes.

> The Pawnee . . . cut the hair close to the head except a ridge from the forehead to the crown where the scalp-lock was parted off in a circle, stiffened with fat and paint, made to stand erect, and curved like a horn, hence the name Pawnee, derived from *parika,* horn.[3]

Cutting the hair to leave only a ridge is sometimes called *roaching.* The Otos, the Osages, and other southern Siouan tribes plucked the

Figure 31. Crow hair styles. Adapted from Norman Feder, "The Crow Indians of Montana," *American Indian Hobbyist*, Vol. V (1959).

entire head or burned the hair off with a glowing stick except for the scalp lock. Some Sioux said the same hair style was common among them long ago.

Blackfoot men sometimes wore a lock of hair down to the bridge of the nose, with the rest of the hair loose. This frontal lock was also described for Mandan men and is seen in drawings by Bodmer and by Catlin of the Assiniboins, Sioux, Hidatsas, Mandans, Arikaras, Kutenais, Nez Percés, and Kiowas.[4] Crow hair styles illustrated in Figure 31 only scratch the surface of possibilities. Note the small braids in front of the ears in two illustrations; these were points of attachment for "Crow bows," to be discussed later.

Braided "knots," or buns, were also known, having been reported for Crees, Assiniboins, Blackfeet, and Mandans, and for Hidatsa medicine men.[5] The bun could be directly over the forehead or at the top of the head, depending on the tribe. Keepers of the sacred pipes among the Gros Ventres could not cut their hair, so it was "worn tied in a bunch just above the forehead."[6]

Catlin's drawing of several Chippewas illustrates variation within a single tribe. (Figure 32)

Symbolic cutting of children's hair occurred among the Omahas; the style of cut depended on the heritage of the father. (Figure 33)

Small objects were often used to decorate the hair.

> Bunches of feathers and other objects tied upon the head are survivals of an immediate past in which they had a value other than decorative. . . . The use of eagle feathers on the head (among the Blackfeet) seems much less pronounced than among the Dakota, the inclination being [for the Blackfeet] to use strips of ermine and bunches of owl feathers. . . . According to Maximilian a small shell was often suspended over the temple.[7]

Generally, men had more elaborate hairdos and more hair ornaments and headdresses than women. Women's hair styles were quite simple, with a center part and two braids being the commonest fashion.

Figure 32. Chippewa (Ojibwa) hair styles. From a lithograph by George Catlin, 1835. Courtesy of the Public Archives of Canada.

While some tribes were careless in hair grooming, individuals in other tribes oiled their hair every morning with bear grease. Castoreum and sweet-smelling herbs were used, as well as cactus pith rubbed on to give a glossy effect. Soapwort (bouncing Bet) and yucca suds were used for cleansing.[8] Primitive brushes were made from wrapped bundles of spear grass, horsehair, or porcupine hair, or of sticks carved of wood, before early traders introduced brass combs.

Hair coloring was not exclusively a Caucasion custom. Painting the hair was usual among the village Indians. Crees used paint sparingly and the Assiniboins regularly. Among the Prairie tribes, colored clays and, when available later, vermilion were often put in the hair, especially along the part(s). Hidatsas sometimes dressed the back of the hair with white clay, while the Gros Ventres usually

92

Figure 33. Omaha haircutting. Adapted from Alice C. Fletcher, "Glimpses of Child-Life Among the Omaha Tribe of Indian," *Journal of American Folklore*, Vol. I (1888).

spotted the rear braid with orange pigment. Assiniboins often smeared the hair with clay in front. The long hair pieces mentioned earlier were often colored with dabs of a pinkish-colored clay or spruce gum. These hair pieces were common among the Crows, Mandans, Blackfeet, Arikaras, Gros Ventres, Western Sioux, Arapa-

Figure 34. Typical hair bow. The wooden pin holding this particular bow to the pigtail is decorated with plumes and two whorls of fluffs. The peg is wrapped with beads between the fluffs.

hoes, Kiowas, Comanches, Cheyennes, Nez Percés, Hidatsas, and Assiniboins.[9] They were either added to the end of existing hair (the custom in most tribes) or used as a separate decorative device tied to the head (Blackfeet). The top, where the hairpiece was attached by a thong around the forehead, was covered with a horizontal piece of quillwork, of beadwork, or vertically hanging ermine tails. The hair was divided into eight to eleven vertical rows, braided or unbraided. At almost three equal intervals, decoration was placed horizontally across. The top horizontal band of the three, and sometimes the middle, or second, band had a thread running through so that the vertical rows of hair were strung together right next to one another. Sometimes large "Crow" beads were placed in between the rows.

Another hair ornament was the "bull's tail." Beaded or quilled, these ornaments are now made from steer tails; earlier they were made from horse tails, with very old specimens constructed from bison tails. The hair was either left natural or dyed a color such as red, purple, green, or yellow.[10] Feathers were sometimes attached to the top of these ornaments. These bull's tails were "general among the Assiniboine, Gros Ventre, Dakota, and the village Indians."[11] (Color Plate V)

"Bows" were observed as a hair ornament by Bodmer.[12] Basically, a bow was cut out of rawhide and slipped into a tightly wound spiral of sixteenth-inch brass wire. The ends of the bow were covered with beads or dentalium shells, and beads and hair pipes were hung from the lower end of the bow, which was worn vertically. In wearing, a man's small pigtails in front of the ears were slipped into the wire

94

coils, and the ornaments were held in place by forcing decorated wooden pins into the coils. (Figure 34)

Another type of bow was worn by women of the Caddoes, a fringe-area tribe; it probably was introduced from the East. (Figure 35) Harness leather in a bow shape was covered with cloth and the edges beaded. Designs were added with domed metal "spots." A metal band ½ by 3 inches was bent to fit around the middle of this bow and a long ribbon or ribbon-appliquéd cloth was fastened at the bottom (the wider end). Thongs were attached through holes in the end of the metal band to tie this ornament to the hair. The drawing is in proper proportion; the actual pattern was seven inches long.

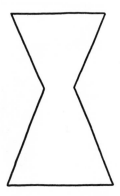

Figure 35. Caddo hair-bow pattern.

Pieces of otter, mink, beaver, or buffalo fur were sometimes wrapped around or plaited into bunches of hair or braids. Similar use was made of trade cloth. Cohoe illustrates an Indian with one braid covered with red and black cloth; the other, red cloth only.[13]

Kroeber depicts a small quilled hoop or "wheel" worn on either side of the head.[14] A similar head ornament had the interior of a hoop rawhide-laced, so that it resembled a lacrosse racket (Figure 36).

Animal-fur caps were common on the Plains. Among the Plains Crees,

> men's winter hats consisted of a ring of buffalo hide, with the hair side outermost. A sinew was threaded along the upper edge and pulled tight to draw the cap to a peak. Another style of headgear was simply a fur fillet some six inches wide . . . of dogskin [or] coyote hide. . . .
> . . . Entire hides of small animals were used as ceremonial headgear in consequence of vision instructions.[15]

Figure 36.   Hair wheels.

White wolfskin caps were worn by Assiniboin men. "[The full war dress among the Nez Percés] consists of the entire skin of a wolf's head, with the ears standing erect, fantastically adorned with bear's claws, bird's feathers, trinkets, and bells." Use of grizzly-bear skins as head covering has been mentioned previously.[16]

Fur crowns were made of the animal furs mentioned above, but by far the most common fur used was that of the otter. Figure 37 shows: *A,* cased otter skin; folded skin is wrapped around the wearer's head, head end (head frequently removed, as shown) slipped into the vent. The tail can be left hanging loose, as in *B,* or folded around as in *C.* Trim can be added, such as diagonal beaded bands, ribbonwork, or a German-silver concha (*D*). In *E,* the head represented by dots was not placed in the vent or cut off, but rather became part of the decoration. The tail was removed and sewed in a different position. The sewing was covered with cloth or with ribbon appliqué; a concha might also be added. All these have been crowns prepared from *cased* skins. If skinned flat (*F*), legs and tail were removed. The skin was folded in half lengthwise, with trade cloth inserted into the fold. The tail was decorated and sewn back on, as in *G.* In *H,* the tail was also folded. The tail could be attached in a

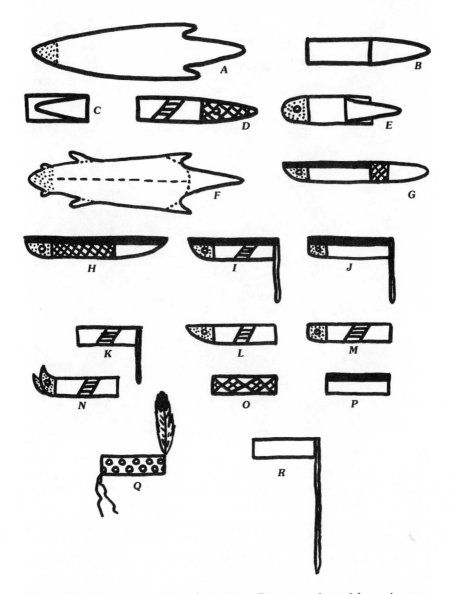

Figure 37. Facing page: Otter-fur turbans. Diagram adapted from descriptions by Norman Feder in "Otter Fur Turbans," *American Indian Tradition,* Vol. VII (1961).

Figure 38. Old Eagle, an Oto photographed in Oklahoma by Edward S. Curtis in 1927. Plate 679 in folio volume XIX of *The North American Indian.* Note the otter-fur turban, peace medal, and grizzly-bear claw necklace.

vertical position with the head left as it was (*I*), head trimmed square (*J*), or head removed (*K*). The tail could be left off as in *L, M,* or *N.* In *N* the head flap was split and thereby doubled. Figure *O* is simply a band of fur; *P* is a folded otter strip with a trade cloth insert revealed at the top of the fold. Figure *Q* is the general Plains type. No two examples are alike, as they were decorated with beaded rosettes, mirrors, ribbons, sequins, feathers, buttons, pendant wolf

98

Figure 39. Plume holder. Longitudinal section of a plume holder of bone in which the quill, or feather shaft, is looped around a thong.

---

tails, or "dime-store" ornaments. The circles in figure 37 represent any of these decorations. Figure *R* is a simple fur band with an entire otter skin hung down the back. Normally *I, J,* and *K* were worn with the tail at the side of the head. Another variation was to wear *K* with the tail at the back.[17]

Cloth trade items were frequently fashioned into head coverings. Catlin mentions "turbans made of vari-coloured cotton shawls, purchased of the Fur Traders." Bandannas, when they were introduced, were worn with a buffalo-bone decorative button by the Comanches.[18] Sashes were also often worn as turbans.

Roaches were common on the Plains:

The custom of shaving the head and ornamenting it with the crest of deer's hair belongs to [the Konzas]; and also to the Osages, the Pawnees, the Sacs, and Foxes, and Ioways, and to no other tribe that I know of. . . . [Catlin painted a Blackfoot wearing a roach, also.] The hair [was] cut as close to the head

99

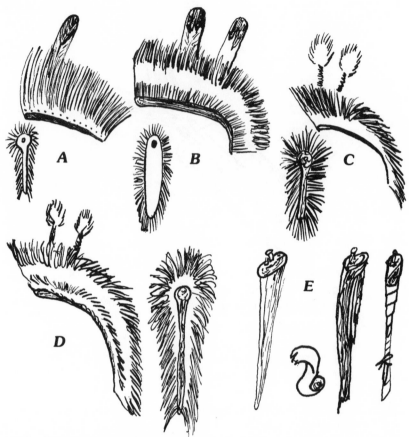

Figure 40. Roaches. Adapted from James H. Howard, "The Roach Headdress," *American Indian Hobbyist,* Vol. VI (1960).

as possible, except a tuft the size of the palm of the hand, on the crown of the head, which is left of two inches in length; and in the centre of which is fastened a beautiful crest made of the hair of the deer's tail (dyed red) and horsehair. [To Catlin's account should be added the frequent use of porcupine guard hair, turkey beard, moose mane, and skunk hair, often surmounted by an eagle quill.] In the center of the patch of hair . . . is preserved a small lock, which is never cut, but cultivated to the greatest length possible, and uniformly kept in braid, and passed through a piece of curiously carved bone [roach spreader]; which lies in the centre of the crest, and spreads it out to its uniform shape, which they study with care to preserve. Through this little braid [scalp lock] and outside of the bone, passes a small wooden or bone key [pin] which holds the crest to the head. . . .[19]

The main purpose of the roach "spreader" is "to provide a firm base of attachment for plume holders" which, in turn, are short cylinders of bone, usually canine femora [also different sorts of bone, wood, metal or, lately, plastic] in which eagle feathers are attached . . . by means of thongs running through a loop in the base of the feather and out through holes in the sides of the plume holder as shown in the cutaway sketch. (Figure 39) Another and perhaps the most common method should be mentioned: the feather shaft is put on a carved bell-bottomed pin which swivels loosely in a bell-shaped socket. This method permits the feathers when not in use to be removed and stored apart from the rest of the roach.[20]

In Figure 40, *A* was common on the southern Plains and perhaps was the earliest type of roach. "The earlier roaches seemed to be the small ones that set back on the head—the deer hair left long in the center."[21] *B* was reported only for the Omahas, Poncas, and Teton Sioux. *C* was common on the central and northern Plains. *D* was worn in the northern Plains Grass Dance (where the dancer does not wear a shoulder bustle which would interfere with this long roach). *E* shows a specially carved stick; the roach is carefully wrapped around the stick, then the two are covered by wrapping with a long strip of cloth or buckskin. Common in the East, the roach was rather uncommon to Plains tribes until shortly after the middle of the 1800's, when it spread rapidly as a "must" for the Grass, or Omaha, dancer.

Eagle-feather bonnets were once uncommon headdresses, with single feathers or plumage of other birds used much more commonly. The origin of this headgear is uncertain, though its spread was certainly related to the use of the horse on the Plains. Though

101

Figure 41. Rawhide sun visor.

Wissler maintains that eagle bonnets were not worn by the Blackfeet, ermine skins taking the place of eagle feathers; nonetheless, the Blackfeet before the 1800's made a "stand-up" bonnet. Basically, this was little more than plumes placed in a rawhide headband. This style of bonnet was also used by all the tribes on the Upper Missouri and northern Plains before it was replaced by the "sun" bonnet; it was retained by the Flatheads, Nez Percés, and Blackfeet after the appearance of the "sun" style.[22]

The Plains bonnet was most closely associated with the Sioux, often being referred to as a "Sioux" bonnet. Whether this tribe originated this headpiece is unknown; "Crow Indians are, by some tribes, given the credit of inventing this headdress."[23] Perhaps it was a natural transition from the Blackfoot "stand-up" bonnet.

The bonnet was constructed with a leather or felt base (crown), which could be covered with fluffies (hackles, or down), split eagle plumes, or fur. Eagle-tail (or wing) feathers were attached in a circle to this. The bottom of each feather might be looped (as in Figure 39), or a leather strip attached; a thong through the natural or the leather loop attached the feathers to the crown. The Plains Crees used wooden pegs; the feather shaft was forced onto a peg and the peg was held in place by sinew binding.[24] The feather's base was often wrapped with red or blue trade cloth. The base might be decorated with plain or dyed fluffies, or feathers from any native bird. Down was dyed, using the same dyestuffs utilized in coloring porcupine quills; colored hackles were also available from early traders. Plume shafts might be decorated with small quill-wrapped strips of rawhide.

Feather tips could be decorated with plain or dyed fluffies, small bunches of horse- or cow-tail hair, or small circlets of leather, or combinations of these. Among some tribes, a quilled or beaded band was placed at the brow. Various pendant objects were placed on the sides (above the ears), including ribbons, fur strips, and ermine pelts (especially on the northern Plains). Mirrors or beaded rosettes (much later) might also be added at these points. Often a "medicine" plume, decorated as the owner wished, was placed in the center of the "sun." Single or double trailers, holding additional feathers, might be added at the back. The caps of some bonnets in the central and north sections were trimmed with white fur and a pair of horns instead of with eagle feathers. Horned bonnets of this type seem to have been used principally, if not exclusively, by medicine men, and are usually called "doctors' bonnets."[25]

Eyeshades, vizors of rawhide or of elk hair, have been reported for the Arapahoes and for the Plains Crees, and were probably used by other tribes as well. This was

> a piece of rawhide somewhat over a foot long. Near the back end of this, a circular area about six inches in diameter has a number of radii slit into it. When this part of the rawhide is pressed upon the top of the head, the two dozen or more sectors yield, and stand up, forming a circle around the head, interpreted as signifying the camp-circle of tents.[26] (Figure 41)

Many times this type of visor was cut from an old parfleche and bore lopsided designs, or was painted in the parfleche manner after being cut from unpainted rawhide. Often these visors were decorated by incision hide carving, the design being the lighter layers of skin under the surface (or paint could be rubbed into the incisions). Other types of visors included a moose-mane circle, a horsehair-fringe circle, bonnet and turban visors of rawhide, and the war-bonnet foundation extended over the wearer's eyes.

Masks were uncommon on the Plains; the only good example of their existence is the Assiniboin Fool dancer's mask.[27]

103

Headbands were quite uncommon, popular opinion to the contrary.

The hat of the Nez Percé women was the gayest portion of their dress. It was fez-shaped and ornamented with woven designs. The bast of Indian hemp (*Apocynum cannabinum* L.), called *kamo*, originally formed the foundation. . . . Beargrass (*Xerophyllum tenax* Nutt.) was much used as a secondary material to carry the design, either in its natural cream color or stained dark brown or yellow. . . . Corn-husk has largely replaced the native material in modern times, and worsted yarns in gay colors have also been substituted for the grass overlay. . . . The designs were almost always entirely arranged in zigzags, with three points at the top and three at the bottom.[28]

Traders hats have been spoken of earlier; one need only look at photographs of Crow or Blackfoot gatherings of this century to see what a profound influence these items have had in the clothing of these and other American Indians. Such hats could be decorated with bands of tin, feathers, ribbons, and so on, as desired by the owner. A Bodmer engraving depicts similar use of a silk top hat.

Modern Sioux women's "hair strings" (braid ornaments) show great diversity in materials—porcupine quills, seed beads, "Crow" beads, tile beads, and so on. Many of the quilled ones consist of a wheel (circle) and dangle.

10. SKINS AND SHIRTS

The hides of several animals were used by Indians of the Plains in making garments. Bison hides gave warmth; antelope and mountain-sheep skins produced a Sunday-best appearance; deer and elk skins provided durability for daily wear. Methods of dressing skins have been well described.[1]

Basically, tissue clinging to the skin was removed by *fleshing*. The hide was evened by *scraping* with an adzlike tool. The same tool was used to remove the hair from the other side of the hide. These two steps were the only ones necessary in making rawhide. The skins could be dressed further by the tanning, or *braining*, operation, in which they were covered with a mixture of cooked animal brains, fat, and liver; powdered yucca (where available); and occasionally a small amount of salt. Liver was not included in the process by Poncas, Omahas, or Otos. After drying in the sun, the hide was saturated with warm water and rolled up overnight. Excess water was squeezed out by *stripping*. The skin was stretched, smoothed (*grained*) by rubbing the surface with a bone, then softened by *working* it back and forth through a rawhide loop. Skins were smoked to enable them to dry soft and pliant after exposure to rain or snow. Hides were smoked in small smoke houses superficially resembling the Plains "sweat lodges."[2] Taylor gives some average hide sizes: deer, 5 feet 4 inches from head to tail; prong-horned antelope, 4 feet 2 inches; Rocky Mountain goat, 3 feet 4 inches.[3]

One of four stitches might be used in binding skins or, later,

105

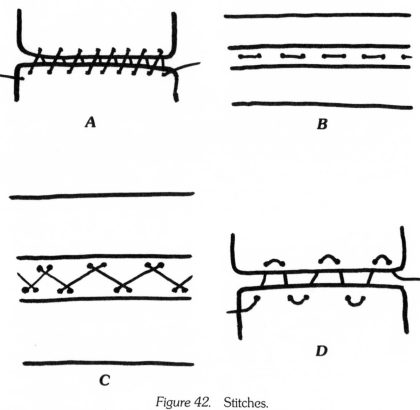

Figure 42. Stitches.

cloth together (Figure 42): A, over and over, used for all seams and in moccasin making; B, running, commonly used in attaching borders and bands to larger pieces; C, mending, used as the name of the stitch implies; D, back and forth, used as an ornamental stitch by the Blackfeet.

Often garment pieces were not trimmed. The yoke of the "two-skin" dress, which will be discussed in more detail later, may have been one result. Sinew was used in stitching skins. Holes were made with a bone awl, the sinew serving as its own needle. Moistened, it was quite flexible and very durable.

Weaving was quite rare among Indians of the Plains proper.

Blankets were made from woven strips of rabbit fur by many Plateau tribes. Sacred-bundle wrappings were of woven buffalo hair. The Omahas are credited with pre-Columbian woven belts. The Nez Percés wove bags and hats from Indian hemp, working in designs with bear grass, cornhusk, or yarn. Plaiting occurred in some quill-work on the Plains.

Cleaning of hides by their Indian owners resembled the use of Fuller's earth nowadays; moist clays of suitable color were rubbed on and when dry brushed off. Gypsum (derived by heating native selenite, a large clear crystalline gypsum) might take the place of clay. Hides were sometimes stored with sweet grass to keep them fresh-smelling, a custom similar to our use of cedar and cedar-lined chests.

Excess leather was cut into fringe. Among the Kiowas and Co-manches, fringes were often long and the strands twisted, resembling cord. Longer fringes on Blackfoot, Cheyenne, and Crow garments were also twisted.

Perhaps the best hide preparation was carried out by the Hidat-sas and the Crows, whose robes and other articles "were conspicuous for their beauty."[4] Blackfoot smoking of skins produced a very dark effect, perhaps resulting in the "black foot" appellation. The staining of the surface of an entire skin or of a finished article of clothing was a frequent occurrence on the Plains.

Robes and robelike articles were common as wearing apparel. In this category should be placed mantles, cloaks, ponchos, and coats, as well as true robes. The definition of each is based on the method of wearing; therefore, the same article may, at different times, be called by different names. A mantle was worn around the body, under one arm and over the other shoulder. A cloak was draped over both shoulders and held in place by tying or knotting in the front. A poncho is a garment with a slit in the middle for the head. A coat is a tailored, shirtlike garment; it was prepared from the same raw materials as the other articles named. A true robe was wrapped around the body and held in place by tucking, belting, or holding with the hand. It was neither pinned nor tied. Mantles per se have not been recorded for any Plains tribe.

Front-tied cloaks have been reported for the Chippewas, the

Arapahoes, and the Osages; among the latter two they were a badge of office in certain men's societies. But they were certainly quite uncommon among these and other Plains tribes.[5]

Simple draped ponchos have been reported for certain Plateau tribes and for the Caddoes. They undoubtedly were the predecessors of the poncholike shirts to be described later.[6]

Coats ("tailored shirts") were introduced by whites. Indian manufacture probably began in eastern Canada in the early 1800's. Tribes in the United States were wearing coats and jackets in the later 1800's.[7] (Color Plate VI)

The true robe, usually of bison hide in the winter and of deerskin in the summer, was universally worn on the Plains. It "was an absolute clothing necessity" for the Mandans and, needless to say, for other northern tribes as well.[8] The woman's robe with quilled or beaded stripes was the only type of robe that was decorated without paint. Men applied painted pictographic designs to their robes. (Figure 43) The hair was left on for winter wear. Almost always, the head of the hide was worn to the wearer's left and the tail to his right. The right arm was exposed and free. The left arm, completely under the robe, often held the robe to the body.

Shirts were worn prior to 1840 by the Assiniboins, Gros Ventres, Blackfeet, various Plateau tribes, Crows, Mandans, and Western Sioux—but, in all cases, for ceremonial use by tribal leaders only.

Deerskin was the hide considered most suitable for shirts; antelope skins are practically synonymous with deerskin; bison

---

Figure 43. Facing page: Men's pictographic designs. *A:* enemy camp, the tripods representing lodges; *B:* enemy war party entrenched in a hole; *C* 1, 2, 3: three ways of representing the taking of a picketed horse from an enemy camp; *D:* horse taken in an open fight; *E:* trade blanket taken from an enemy; *F:* gun taken from an enemy; *G:* bow taken from an enemy; *H:* quiver taken from an enemy; *I:* shield taken from an enemy; *J:* two ways of showing an enemy killed; *K:* enemy's scalp taken; *L:* painter who served as leader of a war party; *M:* painter who served as a war-party scout. Adapted from John C. Ewers, *Blackfeet Crafts* (Lawrence, Kansas, Bureau of Indian Affairs, 1945).

was inclined to be too coarse, and elkskin too thick; those tribes near the Rockies sometimes used the bighorn, i.e., Blackfeet . . . Crow [and Plateau] . . . for ceremonial regalia.[9]

The average shirt was about three feet long, although shirts made from bighorn skins were longer. Shirt sleeves were generally arm-length. This is, of course, extreme generalization. Men's and boys sizes and styles varied with tribe and time.

The sides and sleeves were unsewn in early shirts and loosely sewn, laced, or attached with thongs later; the most recent shirts have completely sewn sides and sleeves. Often the sleeve forearm was sewn, upper arm unsewn, producing what might be called a "half sleeve." A drawstring or tie strings were occasionally placed at the neck opening.

The shirt was usually cut as shown in Figure 45; the tail was often left on. The dotted lines in the right-hand figure represent sewing or lacing. The leg portions were often fringed.

The neck flaps, perhaps suggested to the Indians by the head on the animal hide, were either triangular or rectangular and, if not made from the hide itself, were of red and/or blue trade cloth. Flaps were generally fringed and often either quilled, beaded, or decorated with pendant ermine tails. Rectangular flaps are characteristic of Blackfoot and Assiniboin shirts, but are also found in Crow, Sioux, Nez Percé, and Shoshoni garments. A large disk ("rosette") in quill-work—later, beadwork—was commonly worked on the chest and back of shirts with the rectangular flap; "this decoration was considered most characteristic of the Assiniboine and was said by other tribes to have originated amongst them."[10] A square quilled panel might also be attached in the same area of the shirt. Taylor described a Blackfoot shirt with such panels, each about ten inches square.

Among the Nez Percés, according to Spinden, "the entire [shirt] front was often decorated with small punctuations, usually round and not arranged to bring out any design or figure. Over the shirt was often worn a collar consisting of an entire otter . . . skin, the tail hanging down in front." The Nez Percés used "salmon-colored tanned deerskin."[11] Puncturing as a decoration was found

Plate 1. Mandan bison robe. Courtesy of the Museum of the American Indian, Heye Foundation, New York City.

Plate 2. Blackfoot dress. A beaded buckskin dress from Montana. Courtesy of the Museum of the American Indian, Heye Foundation.

Plate 3. Ute beaded shirt. Note the metal conchas on the long triangular flap. Courtesy of the Museum of the American Indian, Heye Foundation.

115

Plate 4. Facing page: Osage woman's costume. This is one of a number of costumes displayed by Frederick Douglas, of the Denver Art Museum, in an "Indian Fashion Show" held a number of years ago in Buffalo, New York, under the auspices of the Buffalo Museum of Science.

116

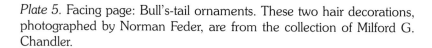

Plate 5. Facing page: Bull's-tail ornaments. These two hair decorations, photographed by Norman Feder, are from the collection of Milford G. Chandler.

Plate 6. Sarsi coat. A painted and quilled buckskin coat from the Sarsis of Canada. Courtesy of the Museum of the American Indian, Heye Foundation.

Plate 8. Ghost dance shirt. Copied from James Mooney, "The Ghost Dance Religion and the Sioux Outbreak of 1890." Bureau of American Ethnology *Fourteenth Annual Report* (1896).

Plate 9. Oklahoma fancy dancer. This photograph of Johnny Whitecloud was supplied by Tyrone H. Stewart, of American Indian Crafts and Culture, and is used with his permission.

Figure 44. The back of a quilled and painted Mandan shirt collected by George Catlin in 1832. Many other items collected by this artist on his travels were destroyed by insect or fire damage. Photograph courtesy of the Smithsonian Institution. Students of the "hide period" should examine Catlin and Bodmer paintings and old documented museum specimens such as this in detail.

127

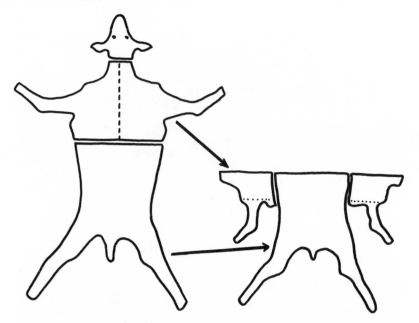

Figure 45. Preparing a war shirt. Adapted from Clark Wissler, "Costumes of the Plains Indians," American Museum of Natural History *Anthropological Papers,* Vol. XVII (1915).

among the Blackfeet as well as the Nez Percés. Widespread use of the shirt is comparatively recent on the Plains and ornamentation styles were "cosmopolitan."

In the north, quilled or beaded bands were often placed over the shoulders, and sometimes along the sleeves. Early bands were narrower (an inch and a half to two inches) and placed over the shoulder seams almost vertically. Later (about 1860), bands were three inches wide, averaging about twenty-one inches long. Two-thirds of the band or strip was worn in front of the shoulder seam and it was placed on the shirt at more of an angle. Modern bands are as wide as four inches and up to forty inches in length.

Sometimes the entire shirt might be painted or stained. The Western Sioux often colored the top half blue and the bottom yellow

Figure 46. Cheyenne quilled shirt. A buckskin shirt from Kansas collected by the Haworth Indian School (F. W. Clarke) in 1894. The bands on the sleeves and over the shoulders match the decorated neck flap in design, color, and quillwork technique used. Courtesy of the Smithsonian Institution.

129

Figure 47. Plains Cree man. Such clothing as he wears is decorated with painted and/or perforated "tadpole" designs. The headdress is of crow feathers. Adapted from a display in the Field Museum of Natural History in Chicago.

(or occasionally green). Among some tribes, the entire shirt was painted reddish-brown as a rejuvenation treatment when the garment had been worn for a long time.[12] Horizontal parallel lines—black, blue, or perhaps green or red—were sometimes painted onto shirts, often in an area that had a base coat of yellow, red, blue, or other-color stain. Colored circles of varying sizes might be used as accents to other ornamentation or as the only decoration. Life forms—bison, bison skull, otter, and so on—were painted onto Plateau and older northern Plains shirts. The Blackfeet were especially fond of a design variously called the "tadpole" and the "bullet." The same design occurs on a Plains Cree shirt observed in the Field Museum in Chicago. (Figure 47) Ghost Dance shirts in particular bore such symbolic devices. A small section of fringing on the elbow was rather characteristic of southern Plains shirts. Often the forelegs were cut into long fringes at the shoulders. Fringing occurred among all Plains tribes.

According to Salomon:

Like the war bonnet, the war shirt trimmed with hair or weasel skins was considered to have great medicine power and could be worn on special occasions only by men in authority or those who had distinguished themselves in battle. Though called scalp shirts by the whites, the hair used in trimming the shirts did not always come from enemy scalps. Each lock on the shirt represented a *coup* won by capturing a horse, taking prisoners, getting wounds, or saving the life of a friend.[13]

In the decoration of a "scalp shirt" hair was divided into small bunches; hair from white men was not used. Such clumps of human hair, scalp locks, or bunches of natural or dyed horsehair were often quill-wrapped at the attachment end; they were attached to shirt seams and along decorative bands. The same treatment might be given by Blackfeet and Crows to ermine (weasel) tails, and hair bundles and weasel tails were often applied in combination.[14]

Dyed down (often red or green), brass beads, teeth, shells, metal studs, and other items found their way onto shirts. Ribbon was sometimes used as a binding around the neck opening.

Introduction of cloth shirts by traders marked the end of the "hide period" generally, but introduced the shirt among Kiowas and Comanches, who had not worn shirts previously.

Calico shirts were early trade items, flannel shirts becoming available later. Both were worn as everyday wear by the Blackfeet in the 1850's. By the 1890's, moccasins were the only vestige of hide clothing in many tribes. White shirts appear to have been no more common as trade items than ready-made shirts of other colors; they were much used during the Ghost Dance craze of the 1870's and 1880's, often being painted with lifelike symbols, usually in black paint.[15] Ghost Dance shirts could be ready-made or home-made. Cloth-shirt styles were dictated by the white man's styles of the times. Collarless shirts and pin-striped shirts were common around the turn of the century.

An Osage was photographed with a floral beaded vest in 1885.[16] "Since about 1890, beaded vests have been worn by Plains men, often as part of a dancing costume . . . derived from European vests. The beaded vest became popular among the . . . Oglala Sioux about . . . 1875. Partly quilled vests were also made, especially by the Sioux.[17] Black-silk tuxedo vests were also sometimes worn by Indians.

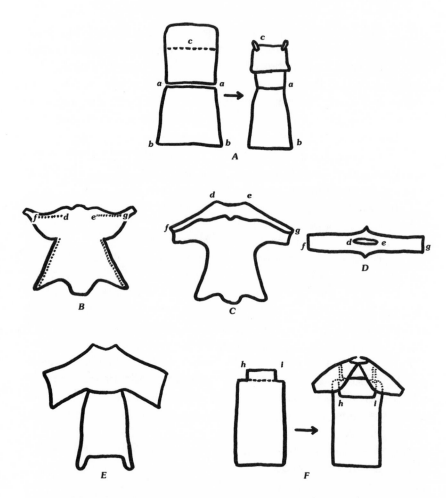

Figure 48. Women's dress patterns in hide. Adapted from Richard G. Conn, "A Classification of Aboriginal North American Clothing," Master's thesis, University of Washington, 1955.

11. DRESSES

Several types of garments were worn by women in the Plains area. The simplest garment was a wrap-around skirt, formed from one hide (or piece of cloth), belted or tied around the waist, and is reported for Caddoes, Iowas, Kansas, Omahas, Osages, Pawnees, and Cheyennes. Patterns for other garments are shown in Figure 48, as adapted from Richard Conn. The "one-sleeve" dress, A, was formed by joining two skins horizontally rather than vertically and was, therefore, considered a "one-skin" garment by Conn.[1] It was worn by Cheyenne, Eastern Sioux, and Plains Cree women, historically overlapping the old northern Plains dress.[2]

The two-skin dress per se was formed by joining two skins, one forming the front and one, the back, as illustrated in B and C. In actual practice the skins were often cut straight at the top and sewed together without the excess-leather "flaps," or—and this was probably the most common method—a yoke, as diagrammed in D, was added. The yoke form differs from the three-skin dress, E, only in the size of the top skin (poncho or yoke). The two-skin dress was worn by Shoshoni, Chippewa, Iowa, Crow, Omaha, Hidatsa, Mandan, Arikara, and Blackfoot women (see Color Plate 7).

The three-skin dress, E, was worn by Utes, Pawnees, Arapahoes, Cheyennes, Western Sioux, Poncas, Kiowas, and Comanches. The top skin might be completely separate from the bottom (a blouse and skirt, if you will), or they might be loosely laced together or fully sewn together.

A two-skin old northern Plains dress, *F*, sometimes called a "jumper" or "slip-and-sleeve" combination, was worn by Assiniboins, Crees, and Chippewas. A short blouselike version worn in combination with a wrap-around skirt was the "old-style" woman's garment among the Blackfeet, Cheyennes, and Pawnees. In general, the jumper, *F*, dress style seems to have been worn over a wider geographical area and for a longer period of time than the side-seam dress, *A*.[3]

Wissler wrote:

> It would be interesting to follow up the problem as to the more specific origin of the Blackfoot form of dress. . . . From structural and geographical points of view, there must be a historical relation between the inserted top piece of the Blackfoot yoke [*D*], the attached cape-like yoke of the Western Sioux, etc. [*E*], and the folded-over "yoke" of the Cree [*C* or *F*]. The separate cape of some Shoshone and other southern tribes [blouse and skirt] may be accounted for as a special differentiation or an independent feature afterward entering into the dress. While we need more data, the distribution is suggestive; the separate cape in the south, the heavy combined cape and skirt in the middle, the lighter more sleeve-like cape in the north.[4]

It could also be theorized that the sleeves of the old northern Plains "slip-and-sleeve" dress led to the invention of the "two-skin" dress with set-in yoke.

Sleeves were capelike and often not true sleeves, not being sewn together all the way down. They were of varying lengths and widths. Sometimes, sleeves were loosely tied together at the bottom with thongs. Crow sleeves were true sleeves, sewn completely together; they were often rather tight-fitting. Generally, Arapaho and Cheyenne dresses had square-cut cape extensions. The Western Sioux had a characteristic notched sleeve. The neck was cut low among the Kiowas, Comanches, and the Utes.

Cloth used in early dresses was strouding—usually blue, but also scarlet red and, later, green and yellow. Calico was somewhat popular. Sateen—a satiny cotton—was introduced in the late 1800's.

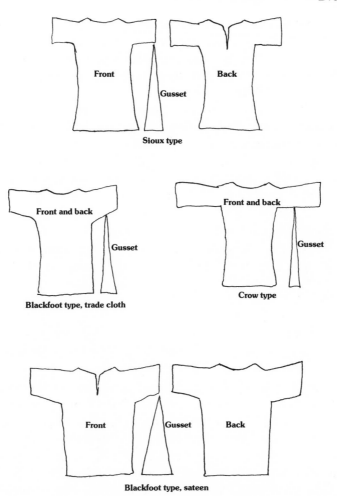

Figure 49. Women's dress patterns in cloth. Adapted from Bill Holm, "Plains Indian Cloth Dresses," *American Indian Hobbyist,* Vol. IV (1958).

Cloth-dress patterns were somewhat more square-edged, as seen in Figure 49. The Sioux-type dress has a long gusset panel and square "wings." Crow dresses had longer, narrower, closed sleeves. Sateen dresses had a wider gusset and completely sewn sleeves, as compared to dresses of trade cloth (strouding). Velvet was also used by

135

the Blackfeet. The modern Crow hide dress is patterned after wool dresses, not after old hide dresses. The same is true for the cut of some contemporary Sioux rectangular-yoke hide dresses; they are cut like the remembered old woolen dresses, not like the too-old-to-be-remembered hide dresses.

Trinkets such as bells, deer hooves, thimbles, buttons, sequins, coins, rhinestones, claws, fluffies, metal disks, brass "spots," tinklers, and so on, were sewn on—primarily according to definite tribal styles, but also, to some extent, to suit the whim of the wearer. The use of elk teeth was common to all tribes, but especially to the Crows, who used them extensively; other tribes made sparing use of them. Cowrie shells or teeth carved from bones were substituted occasionally for the elk teeth.

Dentalium, cowrie, and olivella shells were often used to decorate dresses. The most typical decoration on an old cloth dress of the Western Sioux was concentric rings of dentalia.[5] Sioux skin dresses often had fully beaded yokes. The Blackfeet and Plateau tribes often used horizontal bands of beadwork, quillwork, or ornaments. Beaded bands were alternately of light- and dark-colored beads (blue and white, black and white, light blue and dark green, pink and dark green, and so on). Plateau tribes worked designs into these bands. In addition to the bands themselves, the Blackfeet often attached thongs at the top (under the bands) and pendant thongs and bead-rimmed patches of red and/or black cloth at the bottom of their skin dresses. Usually cloth patches at the center of the front and back were triangular pieces (symbolic of a bison skull or perhaps of the uterus), and ones on each side were rectangles.

On the southern Plains decoration, if there was any, was limited to narrow painted or beaded edgings. Because of the difference in construction (three skins), beaded rosettes or other ornaments were often placed on the lower skins of the garment at or below the seam.

12. LEGGINGS

Generally, men's "leggings reached from the ankle to the thigh and were held in place by tying thongs, attached to their tops, to the belt (or by attaching the hind legs to the belt). Leggings were not worn all the time."[1] As in shirts, the most frequently used material was deerskin, especially on the eastern Plains; however, leggings of antelope, Rocky Mountain goat, and elk hide have been reported.

The earliest leggings were probably just folded-over animal skins (*A* of Figure 50), tacked together at their junction. One early legging (*B*) reported from various Prairie and Eastern tribes had the seam worn in the front. According to Feder:

> Across the Plains from the Mandan to the Jicarilla Apache, the same pattern for the front-sewn legging is worn as a side-sewn legging. . . . Among such peoples as the Winnebago, the front-seam legging is said to be the older form. . . . If this is correct, the distribution of this pattern . . . may indicate that the front-seam legging had a wider distribution than at present. . . . If the side-sewn legging did replace the front-sewn legging on the Plains, as it seems to have done, one wonders if the change was influenced by the introduction of riding, as a matter of convenience to the rider. Long leggings of either type were worn by men. However, in the Plateau . . . women [of some tribes] also wore them.[2]

137

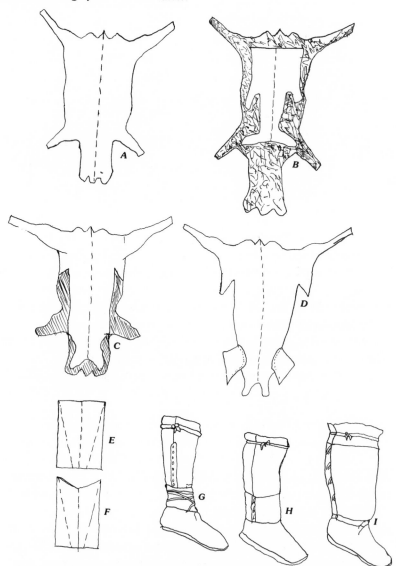

Figure 50. Legging patterns and styles. Adapted from Norman Feder, "Bottom Tab Leggings," *American Indian Tradition*, Vol. VIII (1962); and Richard G. Conn, "Blackfeet Women's Clothing," *American Indian Tradition*, Vol. VII (1961).

The side-sewn legging might be just a simple sewn hide (A), or could be cut with bottom tabs as in C. The excess foreleg portion might be completely removed, fringed, allowed to drape as an extra long flap, or added as a gusset, as shown in D.

> When worn, the legging of this style usually fits extremely tightly to the leg. Many of them are so narrow that it is often impossible for a European to put them on. . . . The foreleg hide of the animal tends to drag behind the wearer. . . . Careful examination of Bodmer's paintings, however, reveals that [these legs] were tied around the ankle. . . . It seems unlikely . . . that the flaps were left free.[3]

The exact "cut" depended on the shape and size of the skin used.

Bottom-tab leggings have been reported for the Western Sioux, Otos, Omahas, Poncas, Mandans, Pawnees, Nez Percés, Crows, Blackfeet, Utes, Assiniboins, Arikaras, and Iowas. "Most of the Plains tribes had stopped using bottom tab leggings sometime before the reservation period but . . . the style did carry over for special use of chiefs among the Omaha, Ponca and Pawnee right into the start of the 20th Century."[4]

Perhaps one of the earliest uses of strouding was in leggings, hide shirts being worn in combination with the much-preferred cloth legging. The earliest legging pattern in cloth was a simple sewn rectangle, as in Figure 50E. Later, a V-cut was made, as in F.

In many tribes, the women wore leggings from the ankle to above the knee; leggings of the Assiniboins, Northern Shoshonis, Mandans, Plains Crees, Hidatsas, and Teton Sioux were from the ankle to the knee only.[5] The woman's legging was kept in place by a garter (thong, otter-fur strip, or gartering from the trader) tied around the leg above the calf. In some tribes women turned the ankle flap of the moccasin up over the legging, while in others, especially in the south, they made the moccasin and legging in one piece. This style perhaps arose among the Comanches; it is now found among Kiowas, Comanches, Utes, Cheyennes, and Arapahoes.[6] Some of these southern boot-moccasins had a long flap which hung from the knee to the middle of the calf.[7]

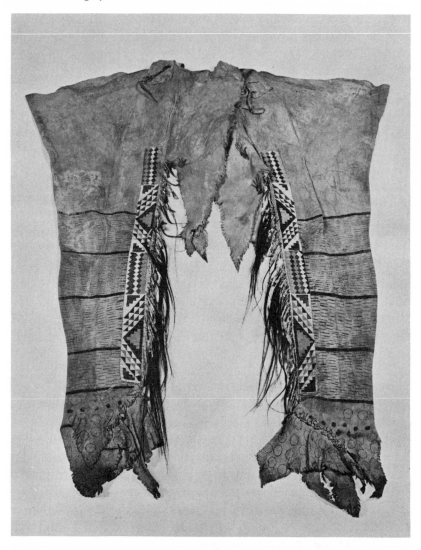

Figure 51. Pawnee leggings. These are bottom-tab leggings from the F. W. Clarke Collection (1894). The strips are loom-beaded. Painted decorations include small painted hands on the top flaps; brown lines are continuous around the leggings; there are dots and circles on the bottom tabs. The fringes are of human hair wrapped with purple porcupine quills. Courtesy of the Smithsonian Institution.

140

Three kinds of Blackfoot women's leggings (same types observed throughout the northern Plains) are *G, H,* and *I* of Figure 50; *G* is the simplest kind, practically undecorated. It was sewn into a tube at the top, buttoned at the bottom. *H* is a skin or cloth tube with a beaded panel at the bottom (horizontal beaded rows); the panel is closed with tie strings. *I* is the type most commonly worn today; it is a trapezoidal piece of beadwork (vertical beaded lanes) with a skin or cloth top flap. It is never sewn closed and might be called a "wrapped legging."

During the period of White-Indian contact along the Northern Plains, a short wrapped legging, called a "saver," was often worn by White (males) . . . over cloth trousers. . . . The Winnebago form of wrapped legging is similar to the saver. . . . The Winnebago legging, like most knee-length leggings in Indian North America, is worn by women only[8] [Figure 52].

Like other clothing, decoration of leggings was quite varied, depending on the maker, tribe, and time. Painting, quilling, beading, and fringing were all common. Metal objects, shells, feathers, human hair, and horsehair—dyed (yellow very common) or natural—might be attached. The hair was often quill-wrapped. Decorations on a woman's leggings often represented honors given her husband.

Following are some tribal characteristics of legging decoration.

Western Sioux: bottom tabs were short or absent.

Crows and Nez Percés: quill-wrapped horsehair was frequent as decoration. Fringed bottom tabs and cloth panels were common. Rocky-mountain goatskins were used often.

Blackfeet: pericardium was usually used instead of sinew to tie scalp locks. Large areas were painted black; ermine skins or ermine tail fringes were common.

Assiniboins, Crees: fringes were quill-wrapped at the base.

Poncas, Omahas: green painting or staining was employed. Round dots were punctured into chiefs' leggings. Scalp locks were frequent.

Mandans, Otos, Omahas: feathers were placed in the fringe.[9]

141

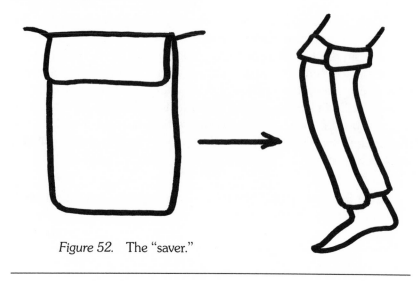

Figure 52. The "saver."

Southern Plains: fringes were twisted and hides painted.

Many old leggings are painted with dark brown (bog-iron ore) stripes. Brown maidenhair fern stems were also often used to create these stripes. Bird or porcupine quillwork was in natural, yellow, or orange (bloodroot); later, red and blue derived from strouding were added. Perforation of costume pieces as a method of decorating slowly went out of style after 1830.

Quilled strips similar to those used as shirt decoration were common as decoration on old men's leggings. Among the Western Sioux, they were gradually replaced by beaded strips in the period of 1870 to 1890. "Panels" of either cloth in contrasting color (bordered with ribbons or with lanes of beadwork) or beaded rectangles were used on legging bottoms. Such "panel" leggings were especially popular among the Crows, but were also worn by Blackfeet and various Plateau tribes. Bottom panels appeared among the Western Sioux after 1890, as did large rosettes on Sioux legging bottoms.[10]

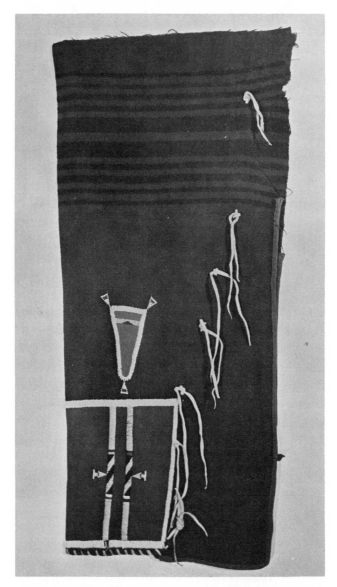

Figure 53. Crow bottom-panel cloth legging.
Courtesy of the Museum of the American Indian, Heye Foundation.

143

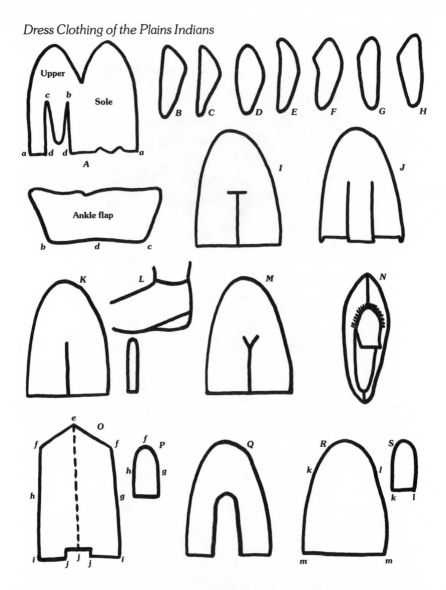

Figure 54. Moccasin patterns. Adapted from Julian H. Salomon, *Book of Indian Crafts and Indian Lore* (New York, Harper, 1928); Dennis Evans, "Southern Plains Women's Boots," *American Indian Tradition,* Vol. VIII (1962); and Clark Wissler, "Material Culture of the Blackfoot Indians," American Museum of Natural History *Anthropological Papers,* Vol. V (1910).

13. FOOTWEAR

Two basic types of moccasins were worn in the Plains area: one with a soft sole (same as the upper); the other, with a hard (often raw elkhide) sole (different from the upper). The most common soft-soled moccasin was a side-sewn moccasin, the pattern for which is shown in Figure 54A. This was the moccasin worn until the 1870's or 1880's on the northern Plains. It persisted there in winter foot-wear made of bison hide worn with the fur on the inside, and is still worn by various Plateau tribes. Side-sewn moccasins were worn by Crees, Nez Percés, Sarsis, Assiniboins, Blackfeet, Gros Ventres, Shoshonis, and Crows.[1]

In hard-sole moccasins, soles were cut to conform to foot pattern generally. Chief Noisy Owl of the Oglala Sioux made drawings, however, showing the distinctive tracks (soles) of several tribes, as shown in Figure 54: B, Western Sioux; C, Cheyenne; D, Arapaho; E, Crow; and F, Pawnee. To this can be added patterns for Kiowas, G, and Comanches, H. This should, of course, all be taken with a grain of salt — the implication is that all the members of a tribe have feet of the same contour, which is an absurdity.[2]

Uppers might be cut in a variety of patterns. Perhaps the most common was that shown in Figure 54I. A tongue was cut to match the top of the T. The pattern is reversed for the opposite foot. In J, the tongue and upper were cut as one. This pattern was found in certain Sarsi, Blackfoot, Gros Ventre, Western Sioux, Arapaho, Shoshoni, and Comanche moccasins. In K of Figure 54, the tongue is

145

narrow and carefully stitched in or is omitted; this was observed in Ute moccasins only. A moccasin upper, cut as in *I* but with the sole turned up as in *L*, was observed in certain Shoshoni moccasins.

Some Sarsi moccasins were cut as in *M*; the small triangular flap was the only tongue. A Plains variant of the Eastern pucker-toed soft-sole moccasin is shown in *N*; the pattern, *O*, is the same for both feet, and the tongue, *P*, is cut separately. Piece *O* is folded along the dotted line and lines *e–f* sewn together. Piece *P* is added, matching points *g* and *h* with careful puckering along lines *f–g* and *f–h*. Points *i* were joined and points *j* were joined. This pattern was observed in Chippewa, Cree, Assiniboin, and Eastern Sioux specimens. Moccasins were decorated before sewing, sewn inside out, then reversed (often with difficulty).

In most of these patterns, vertical slashes were made at regular intervals in the upper, slightly below its top, to accommodate thong laces. Often a piece of cloth might be added to mask the thong and provide ornamentation. An extra piece of skin might be stitched at the top of the upper to increase the moccasin height—a so-called ankle flap as shown in *A*. The ankle flap is more common on women's moccasins. In *Q*, an upper, this extra piece is a long rectangle stitched into the U, and the finished product became a boot; probably a Comanche invention, these women's boots have been collected among the Kiowas, Utes, Cheyennes, and Arapahoes as well.[3]

There are northern Plains women's boots also, which can be seen in Saskatchewan, Alberta, North Dakota, and Montana. The old-time high-topped traditional Cree woman's moccasin (*N*) was probably the prototype. However, the modern form has a foot-outline soft sole, not a puckered-around-the-vamp soft sole. Modern Crow women use the same pattern, but with hard soles.[4]

The two-piece soft-sole moccasin, *R* and *S*, may have been more widely distributed on the Plains than Wissler indicates. The edge of piece *R* between the points marked *k* and *l* is sewed to the edge of piece *S* from *k* to *l*. Points marked *m* are brought together and the edge sewed to make the heel seam. The author has a pair

Figure 55. Comanche moccasin (man's left foot). Courtesy of the Smithsonian Institution.

of moccasins (tribe?) with soft soles made within the past decade and conforming to pattern *I*.

Comanche, Kiowa, and, to some extent, Cheyenne moccasins were decorated with fringes. Comanche moccasins had short fringe along the top seam from the laces to the toe and six-to-eight-inch-long fringe, with sometimes fifty or more strands, along the heel seam.[5] Occasionally a skunk tail rather than fringe was attached to the heel. Fringe marks were obvious in Comanche tracks. Fringed moccasins distinguished noted warriors among the Plains Crees.[6] Tails of deer or bison or the "beard" from the bison trailed at the heels of many Cheyenne moccasins.

To summarize basic construction of the hard-sole moccasin: heavy rawhide was cut to conform to the foot outline for the sole. Different patterns have been shown for cutting uppers from deer or

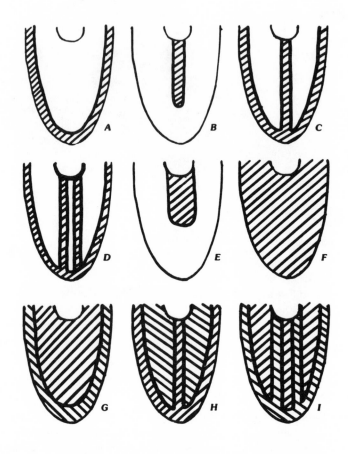

Figure 56 A and B. Moccasin-toe decorations. Figure 56A, *A* to *I*: hatched portions represent beaded or quilled areas. Hatching in differing directions indicates both beading and quilling. Adapted from Clark Wissler, "Distribution of Moccasin Decorations among the Plains Tribes," American Museum of Natural History *Anthropological Papers,* Vol. XXIX (1927). Figure 56B (facing page), *A* to *O:* designs adapted from Alfred L. Kroeber, "Ethnology of the Gros Ventre," American Museum of Natural History *Anthropological Papers,* Vol. I (1908).

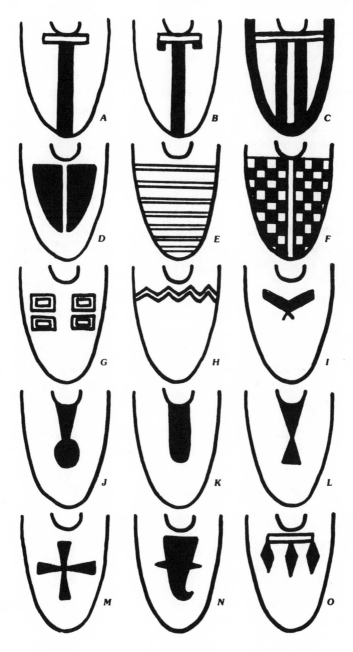

other skins. A tongue, lacing thongs, a "thong protector," ankle flaps, and/or fringes might be added.

In studying moccasin decoration, it should first be pointed out that, regardless of the method of construction, the beaded designs used would remain essentially the same for a particular beadworker in a given tribe. Early decoration consisted of painting and/or quill-work. After its introduction beadwork was used in combination with, or completely replaced, quillwork. Wissler studied 515 geometrically decorated pairs representing the period 1890 to 1915; in 8 per cent the decoration was completely quills; 78 per cent, all beads; and 14 per cent, beads and quills combined. Most moccasins in this series were executed in three or four colors. Preferred colors were yellow, red, green, and purple, but orange, blue, pink, lavender, light purple, and white were also used. White was the preferred background color in beaded moccasins, although the Assiniboins preferred blue backgrounds.[7]

Distributional studies of types of moccasin decoration (Figure 56A) suggest that the largest number of decorative types were used by centrally located tribes (Crows, Western Sioux, Arapahoes); the smallest number by peripheral tribes (Pawnees, Kiowas, Nez Percés, Plains Chippewas, Comanches, and Iowas). *G* was the most popular type, followed in order by *H, E, B,* and *F.* Wissler selected six of the most common designs:

The total number of tribes represented [in his study] was twenty-one, and the number of tribes for each design was found to be as follows:

[Mountains and checker rows]	20
[Triangles]	14
[Crosses]	16
[Forked trees]	9
[Diamonds]	16
[Full of points]	6

These designs are laid on regardless of the decorative type. . . .[8]

Kroeber in an earlier study described fifteen common designs (Figure 56B). He said all of his designs were used by Dakotas and Assiniboins. "Stripe and border designs" *A, B, C,* and *D* were used by Arapahoes, Cheyennes, Utes, and, as edging only, Kiowas and Comanches. Red-quill lines, *E,* and checkers, *F,* were common on Arapaho and Western Sioux footwear. The four squares, *G,* and transverse-zigzag, *H,* were not very common. The chevron, *I,* was known to Cheyennes and Plains Chippewas; with the "keyhole," *J,* it was also very popular with Gros Ventres, Shoshonis, Crows, and Hidatsas. The "keyhole" is so common that one writer added it to Wissler's nine decorative types (Figure 56A). *K* is the so-called "Blackfoot U," typically, but not exclusively, Blackfoot. The tipi, *L,* is infrequent among the Western Sioux and Gros Ventres. The Maltese cross, *M,* is common among the Western Sioux, Cheyennes, and Arapahoes. Wissler reported: "Strictly realistic designs are rare on moccasins, our examples being for the most part birds and most characteristic of the Southern Cheyenne, but even here they are in the minority."[9]

The bird, *N,* was always executed in quills. Feathers, *O,* like *M,* seem to be associated primarily with the central Plains tribes.

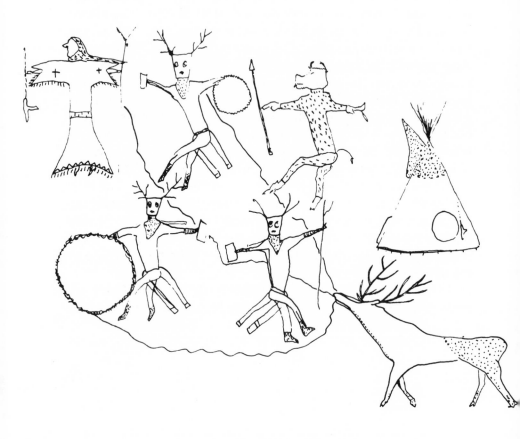

Figure 57. Elk Cult. The drawing depicts members of the Elk Society in costume and masks performing their ritual dance, under the influence of the dream elk. Stamping their feet and flashing sunlight from the mirrors in their hands puts watchers in the power of the cult. An Indian drawing collected by R. Cronau, adapted from Clark Wissler, "Societies and Ceremonial Associations in the Oglala Division of the Teton-Dakota," American Museum of Natural History *Anthropological Papers*, Vol. XI (1912).

14. DANCE AND GROUP COSTUMES

Clothing for use in special dances and ceremonies among the people of the Plains was often unique and always different from everyday dress.

Perhaps the best-known old-time dance typifying the Plains was the Sun Dance. This was an annual ceremony involving most members of the tribe. An affair lasting several days, the Sun Dance was frequently marked by ritualistic self-torture. The men who made the Sun Dance "vow" were painted on the face and body. The dancer wore a whistle fashioned from an eagle-wing bone around his neck. The tortures to which he subjected himself are well described in the literature.

"Each ceremony had special costumes. Membership in various societies was indicated by the wearing of distinctive regalia."[1] Societies had several features in common. All originated in individual experiences or dreams, and each selected its own members. Each tribe had its own group of such organizations. These groups were not static; new groups formed as previous groups became defunct. Men might change groups, often because of new personal revelations. Cults were formed from groups of men venerating particular animals. "Some were disposed to consider the [animal cults] as all parts of one great cult and it is true that they often held their ceremonies at the same time and all jointly participated in the ceremonies of shooting medicine, where they made a show of rivalry." Elk and bear cults were known in many tribes. Among the Oglala Sioux, elk dancers "wear peculiar triangular masks made of young buffalo skins, with a pair of branches trimmed to represent elk's antlers. These horns are wrapped with otter fur to represent horns in the velvet. . . . They carry a hoop of two cross cords, supporting a mirror at the center (Figure 57)."[2]

Bear ceremonialism occurred among Plains Chippewas, Plains Crees, Blackfeet, Assiniboins, Crows, Western Sioux, Cheyennes, Arapahoes, Utes, and Kiowas. "In some areas there were bear cults or classes of medicine men whose souls were thought to dwell within bears' bodies and to activate the bears."[3] The Assiniboins and related tribes offered sacrifices to bears. (For Catlin's painting of a medicine man wearing a bearskin, see Figure 12.)

Certain groups, the *akicita*, were selected to act as a "police force"; one such group among many tribes was the Kit-Fox, or Coyote, Society. Details of costume which might be worn by Kit-Foxes included: (1) coyote jawbone painted red or blue, fastened on an otter band, worn on the forehead; (2) roached hair; (3) wearing of a "hood"; (4) a coyote skin worn as a neckpiece, with the head in front, tail behind, bags of medicine attached to the nose, and the edges, feet, and ears quilled and hung with bells; (5) a crescent badge"; and (6) bodies painted yellow. Table 4 shows tribal distribution of these costume characteristics.[4]

Some *akicita* groups were selected as war leaders because of their bravery in combat. Such groups included the Brave Hearts, the Wolves, and the Dog Soldiers.

> The Arapaho and Cheyenne have each a Dog organization with four scarf-wearing officers pledged to bravery, and characterized by the same ceremonial regalia, such as dew-claw rattles, feather headdresses, and eagle-bone whistles. The union of these logically quite unrelated features in adjoining tribes establishes beyond doubt a common origin."[5]

On the field of battle, the trailing "scarf" of the Dog Soldier was staked with a lance to the ground, where he fought to the death or until another Dog Soldier withdrew the lance.

Most societies were open to men of all ages. However, there

154

TABLE 4. KIT-FOX SOCIETY

Tribe	Features (see text)					
	(1)	(2)	(3)	(4)	(5)	(6)
Hidatsas	X	X				
Mandans	X	X	X			
Assiniboins	X			X		
Teton Sioux	X	X		X		X
Arikaras		X			X	
Cheyennes		X			X	X
Crows		X		X		
Iowas		X				
Poncas		X				X
Blackfeet			X			

were among some tribes groups for older men. "We have in the buffalo dance, the bulls, or old men's society of the Northern Plains."[6]

The Ghost Dance religion can superficially be compared to the Long House religion of Handsome Lake among the Iroquois tribes of New York State. The Plains Ghost Dance and the Iroquois Long House religion are both revivalistic and nativistic. But Handsome Lake reorganized and revitalized existing rituals and cult groups, without creating the limited ends or ideals connected with the Ghost Dance. The Ghost Dance cult existed alongside other native cults, *temporarily*. The Ghost Dance had goals that were immediate and particular; in this, its religious scope was narrower than Handsome Lake's "way." This major influence on the Plains arose with the "prophet" Wovoka, and was popular for perhaps a couple of decades. The massacre at Wounded Knee in 1890 marked both the practical end of Indian-white conflict and of the Ghost Dance and its adherents.

All the men and women made holy shirts and dresses [that] they wear in [the] dance. . . . They paint the white muslin . . . holy shirts and dresses . . . with blue across the back, and alongside of this a line of yellow paint. They also paint in the

front part of the shirts and dresses. On the shoulders and on the sleeves they tied eagle feathers. . . . The ghost dancers all have to wear [an] eagle feather on [the] head. [The shirt] was painted with symbolic figures, among which were usually represented [the] sun [circle], moon [crescent], or stars [morning star, a cross], the eagle, magpie, crow, or sage-hen, all sacred to the Ghost dance among the Sioux.[7] (See Color Plate 8)

Turtles were added to this list of symbols by the Arapahoes; other animals such as bison, otter, and so on, by other tribes.

The ghost dance was but one of a group of . . . ceremonies which . . . became conspicuous because of their diffusion . . . [including] the peyote, the hand game ceremonies, and the grass dance . . . that took their most modern forms during the decades preceding and following the ghost dance [period] [see Figure 26].[8]

The Grass Dance has spread throughout the Plains and is the basis for the "powwow." It is also known as the Omaha Dance by the Sioux; the Wolf Dance among the Shoshonis; the War Dance on the southern Plains; and the Chicken Dance by the Blackfeet. The early Grass dancer wore a porcupine hair (porky) or deerhair type *C* or *D* roach (see Figure 40) with one or two untipped eagle feathers (the porky roach was preferred). He wore an eagle-bone whistle, often in the crude shape of a bird (variously described as a crane, a curlew, or a prairie chicken); no shirt or leggings; a "crow" belt (at least the leader always wore this); a bunch of braided grass attached at the waist, and probably sleigh bells at the knees.[9]

Figure 58. Facing page: "Old-time" Sioux Dancers. The period 1920–35 was marked by the appearance of bustles and bells in profusion. Photographs, ca. 1920's, by the O'Neill Photo Company of O'Neill, Nebraska, by Clarence Ellsworth and others, are often used in costume research by Indian hobbyists interested in this era. They form the basis for drawings by Clyde Feltz, adapted in Figures 59 to 63, in his article "Old Time Sioux Costume," *American Indian Hobbyist,* Vol. IV (1957).

157

Figure 59. "Old-time" Sioux costumes. *A*: skin leggings and skin shirt, breechcloth long in back, short in front. He carries a pipe and pipe bag and wears a simple choker with conch shell and ribbon dangle. There are no rosettes on bonnet, and ribbons serve as bonnet drops. *B*: cloth leggings and skin shirt. He wears trade-cloth hair wraps, silk kerchiefs on knees, knee bells, and hair-pipe breastplate. The fan is of eagle primary-wing feathers. He wears a simple choker with conch and dentalium shells.

Photographs of powwows in the 1920's and 1930's were used by Feder and Feltz in a study of Western Sioux old-time costumes. While the term "old-time" is a misnomer, it is popular among Indian hobbyists to describe older powwow styles. While many of these are rarely seen at modern Sioux powwows, one can still observe examples of old-time clothing: a buckskin "chief's suit" with bonnet; cotton shirt and wool leggings; "long Johns" with bustle; even outfits with no beadwork at all—only sequins, ribbons, rickrack, felt cutouts, and so on. Some of these styles may have longer histories or older antecedents than others and are not exclusively Sioux in distribution.

Three costume styles of the present day have been selected for discussion out of many which exist. The selection was made partly because these styles are perhaps the best known and partly because some writers have described relationships of these styles to the Grass Dance outfit of years ago. The bustleless modern costume of some northern Plains tribes is here compared with the straight dance costume without bustles and the fancy (feather) dance costume with bustles of the southern Plains (Oklahoma).

The costume of the northern Plains dancer began in North Dakota, and its use still centers in that area. The ancestral Grass Dance bustle has been discarded. A feather roach has been replaced with a roach made from auto-choke cables with fluff tips. A head "harness" is worn. This harness has a loom-beaded design on a white background; often there is a small forehead rosette and beaded drops on the sides.

The dancer wears a choker, a silk neckerchief with a German-silver slide, or a beaded collar-tie. A black western-style shirt is standard, with six-inch-long white chainette fringe and rosettes or feather clusters at the shoulders. Beaded "gauntlet" gloves or open-beaded cuffs are part of the ensemble.

A beaded suspender "harness" and loom-beaded armbands, often with beaded rosettes and dangles of beads, ribbons, or fluffs, are worn. Belts are usually four- or five-inch-wide leather straps decorated with loom beading in geometric designs, buckled or tied in the back. The man's breechcloth is of navy blue strouding deco-

Figure 60. "Old-time" Sioux costumes. A: cloth leggings and a pin-stripe cloth shirt of the common "store-bought" variety, with or without cuffs. He wears quilled armbands, earrings, a trade-cloth hair wrap, and ribbons on the braid. He has a large silk kerchief around his neck, with a silver tie slide (usually the kerchief is knotted), a bandoleer bead string, which is usually of hair pipes and brass beads but can be of brass beads by themselves, as shown, or of deer toes (dewclaws) fastened on a leather strap. The bells are fastened on a long strap and wound around the leg below the knee. He has a quilled hair ornament with four stripped feathers. Headbands are

rated in the back with many chevron bands of ribbon. Trousers match the shirt in color and decoration. Five of six large sheep bells or sleigh bells are worn around each ankle now; smaller brass bells over garters were worn below the knees a decade ago. Anklets of white Angora fur are worn. The footwear is usually sneakers.

Women wear a lightweight "informal" cloth dress with the hem from the middle to the top of the knee; sleeves are elbow, three-quarter, or full length. Older women often wear calicoes, while younger people often sport Hawaiian-print dresses. Crow "high boots," often with floral design, and Crow beaded appliqued belts (floral or geometric design) are popular. A princess crown is worn, but far back on the head, not over the forehead as in Oklahoma; the crown is often quilled. A large medallion necklace, quilled or beaded, worn over a fifteen-inch-square neckerchief which is pinned in front, completes the woman's ensemble.[10]

The Oklahoma straight-dancer costume originated with Prairie predecessors. Bustles were worn until the 1930's in some places. The headdress is a roach with spreader and one eagle-tail feather. *Hethuska* feathers hang from the hair over the temples. A white silk hankie is folded to make a narrow headband, knotted over the forehead.

The men wear long bandoleers of brass or aurora borealis beads, hair pipes, and leather spacers; of beads only; or of mescal beans. These often hang to three inches below the waist and have ornaments—feather clusters or bundles of sweet grass (or tobacco

---

rare in these costumes. *B*: cloth leggings and cloth shirt. The breechcloth is decorated with quillwork on the bottom, ribbons, brass sequins, and metallic fringe. The vest is fully beaded. The roach has quilled dangles ending in fluffs. Feathers are not usually trimmed as shown, but this style is sometimes found. The armbands and cuffs are of brass. Silk kerchiefs appear on armbands and hanging from the hair. Earrings are quite common. The sash is the Assumption style. Bells are wrapped around the knees. The bandoleer is made of hair pipes and brass beads. Note the porcupine-guard-hair forehead rosettes. The face paint was common. Normally the dancer would also wear a bustle.

Figure 61. "Old-time" Sioux costumes. A: The trousers and cloth shirt are "store-bought." He wears large forehead fluff and brass beads tied to the hair. The hair is worn loose, not in braids. The choker is of otter fur with a mirror in front. The breast ornament is otter fur with mirrors and a quilled trim. The breastplate is of bones underneath. The back and neck bustles are of matching feathers. The bustle tie is decorated with mirrors. There are three belt dangles of brass studs from a stud belt, all but hidden by the bustle tie. The armbands and cuffs are beaded; the earrings are silver. The knee bells are of solid brass. The breechcloth is decorated simply with

among Peyote members) tied in a silk or taffeta scarf—tied on at the shoulder blade.

A choker of hair pipes and brass or aurora borealis beads with a beaded rosette or a circular piece of conch shell at the center is worn around the neck. Over this, a taffeta or silk scarf, solid-colored (brocades are now popular), is fastened with a German-silver slide.

A collarless solid-color (older) or floral- or paisley-print (modern) shirt with ribbon trim ("ribbon shirt") is worn. While gauntlets or cuffs were worn in the past, they are not part of the apparel of modern dancers. Two trailers, one a dance trailer of ribbon-appliquéd cloth ten inches wide and reaching to the ground, the other a trailer of otter fur two to four inches wide fastened with ribbon to the back of the wearer's neck and also reaching to the ground, are standard for the straight dancer. The otter trailer is variously trimmed, with older trailers also ribbon-appliquéd.[11]

German-silver armbands are always worn. Belts are similar to those of the northern Plains. Finger-woven sashes were extensively used in the Straight Dance costume; shorter, narrower side tabs (drops) done in the same manner and which hang below the shirt hem are now substituted.[12]

Breechcloths are of navy strouding with ribbon appliqué. Leggings match the breechcloth in appliquéd designs and color. Small bells are worn over finger-woven garters, directly below the knees. A straight dancer wears anklets of white Angora goat fur and beaded

---

straight ribbons. *B:* The trousers and shirt are cloth with a cloth fringe, this being common today on the northern Plains. The fringe is of the regular awning type, usually in white on a colored background. Feathers dangle from the roach. He wears large knee bells. The belt is of German silver conchas with a trailer of the same material dangling on the left. The neckpiece is otter fur with a circle of conch shell and ribbons. The bustle spikes have a row of brass hawk bells tied on. The cuffs are brass, and the armbands are beaded. The anklets are of skunk fur (although they could be from an Angora goat, bison, bear, or other animal). The bandoleer is of deer dewclaws.

Figure 62. "Old-time" Sioux costumes. *A*: The trousers are knicker style with high stockings and cloth shirt (knickers were the common leg covering a half-century ago). Note the short haircut. The roach has a fluff dangle. The neck and back bustles are matched. He wears beaded armbands, breechcloth, a concha belt, bells, and fur anklets. The breechcloth has no back flap; there is a bustle trailer. Ribbons, kerchiefs, knee bands, armbands, chokers, bustles, cuffs, and bandoleers would add a lot. *B*: long underwear, either left natural (white or red) or dyed any color. The hair is

Plains hard-sole moccasins. A few wear old-style soft soles appropriate to the tribe with whom they identify. Women wear a cloth blouse and woolen skirt with ribbonwork or beadwork.[13]

The costume of the fancy (or feather) dancer has antecedents on the southern Plains, retaining the Grass Dance bustle. Though the fancy dance began about 1920–22, World War II seems to be the gap between "old-time" and modern costumes in most places, perhaps because of war-time cessation of powwows and slowdown in costume-making, perhaps because of lack of men for singing and for dancing, or for both reasons.

There was a brief period of popularity for an all-feather crest. Popular at present is a roach with spreader and two feathers, especially a roach of deer-tail hair. One recent innovation is a "rocker" spreader that rocks back and forth as the dancer nods his head. A white-silk-hankie headband, knotted over the forehead, is often worn, especially by Peyote members. Around the neck is a choker, loom-beaded or made of hair pipes, and/or a silk neckerchief with a German-silver slide. Beaded gauntlets or cuffs are common. Long hair is "in." The dancer may wear no shirt, a T shirt, or a "ribbon" shirt similar to that described for straight dancers. Capes are coming back into fashion.

A beaded suspender harness is worn, the ends decorated with tassels, fringe or drops, and beaded pendant extensions. Some dancers now wear hair-pipe breastplates.

Additional apparel includes loom-beaded armbands and arm bustles. Belts are similar to those of the northern Plains. There are matching neck and back bustles. A bustle in a U shape is popular,

---

loose down the back, without braids. Stockings, sometimes with garters, are worn. Bells on a long strap are wrapped around the legs below the knees. The breast ornament is otter fur with mirrors and sequin edging. He wears a large silk kerchief around the neck and smaller ones from the armbands. There are matching back and neck bustles, no trailer, and an Assumption sash holding up the bustle. The breechcloth is decorated with a metallic fringe on the bottom, sequins, and ribbon.

165

Figure 63. "Old-time" Sioux costume. He wears long underwear. A few small feathers are attached to the roach spreader. There is a small feather forehead rosette and, at the temple, a mirror, bead, and hair-pipe dangle. Silk kerchiefs are tied to the hair braids. A little quilled side hanging is a part of the bustle ties (a feather cluster might be equally appropriate here). The skunk-fur knee bands are not very common. The armbands and cuffs match in color and design. The bandoleer is made of dewclaws. The feathers attached to his bustle spikes are novel. The hair is braided behind the ears (but could also be braided over the ears).

Figure 64. Straight dancer. Adapted from an undated paper (ca. 1968) by Jerry Smith, "Oklahoma Straight Dancer," California Indian Hobbyist Association.

with extensive use of six-to-seven-inch-long tip fluffies, preferably in the new "fluorescent," or "radiant," colors. Fully or partly beaded or ribbon-appliquéd aprons in what is called "Oklahoma floral" style—designs such as leaves, flags, eagles, stars, and so on—worn over black trunks replace the breechcloth and leggings. The legs are decorated with sheep bells just below the knee and long Angora-fur anklets, or "goats," fastened just a couple of inches below the bells. Plains hard-sole moccasins are worn (see Color Plate 9).

Women wear a white buckskin dress with long fringe or a taffeta dress made in the old style with open sleeves, gussets, and tabs; with both, very typically, a "princess crown" headband is worn. This band often has a single black and white golden-eagle-tail feather in the back. A girl chosen as a princess in a powwow is allowed to wear downy eagle plumes during her "reign." Some girls are trying to introduce modifications of the man's "feather" costume for female wear. Some wear men's outfits at the present time on both the northern and the southern Plains.[14]

Features of modern "Pan-Indianism" cited by James Howard include the War, or Grass, Dance, the fancy-dance and straight-dance costumes, the Stomp Dance (a "follow-the-leader" type), the existence of Indian stores such as that at Pawnee, Oklahoma, and the use of peyote. He feels that mild racial discrimination, a common economic level, the forced use of English, intermarriage, geographic mobility, and school contacts have contributed to Pan-Indianism. The powwow is the secular expression of this movement, while the Native American Church (Peyote Cult) is its religious expression. Howard feels this is the "final stage of progressive acculturation . . . just prior to complete assimilation."[15]

Peyote was acquired by southern Plains tribes between 1850 and 1900. During the twentieth century, its use spread to Canada and California. "Most of the tribes in the United States acquired

---

Figure 65. Facing page: Kiowa skin dress. Collected by Mooney in 1891. This dress is little different from the modern powwow "princess" dress. Courtesy of the Smithsonian Institution.

peyote while on reservations in Oklahoma or from Indians residing there."[16]

The topic of costumes worn by various Indian societies and dance associations on the Plains has only been scratched here. The reader is referred to the bibliography for additional references.

15. COMPARISON AMONG SELECTED TRIBES

Blackfeet

Robe design	Border and box; horizontal stripes
Accessories	Weasel drops; owl feathers in hair
Beading	Overlay predominately; also lazy stitch
Beaded triangle	Checkered
Other designs	Floral designs as early as 1870's
Beads	Basket beads used 1890–1900
Background colors	White predominantly; also light blue
Cloth	Patches common as decoration
Breechcloth	Short in front and back[1]
Metal	Infrequent use on clothing
Hair styles	Frontal lock; bun; hair pieces
Headgear	"Stand-up" bonnet
Shirt	Darkly smoked deer hide; puncturing and tadpole design common; rosettes back and front
Dress	Early, wrap-around; later, two-skin, decorated with horizontal bands of beadwork
Leggings	Often yellow with black horizontal painted stripes; pericardium used in place of sinew to attach scalp locks
Moccasins	Early, side-sewn; decorated with

Blackfoot U, "crooked nose," keyhole,
or cross stripe

Associated tribes	Sarsis, Gros Ventres, Plateau tribes; unfriendly to Plains Crees and Chippewas, their neighbors on the east

Crows

Robe design	Border and box
Accessories	Elk teeth, deer hooves, hair tassels, or feathers on garments; loop necklace
Beading	"Crow" stitch or overlay
Beaded triangle	Long and narrow
Other designs	Early use of floral
Beads	Varied; small preferred
Background colors	Light blue preferred; also lavender
Cloth	Patches sometimes used as decoration
Breechcloth	Long in front
Metal	Tinklers common 1900–10
Hair styles	Pompadour; hair pieces; very long
Headgear	"Sun" bonnet; "Crow bow"
Shirt	Close-fitting and well-made of elkskin
Dress	Two-skin with true sleeves; cloth, narrow-sleeved; elk teeth common as decoration
Leggings	Fringed bottom tabs; quill-wrapped horsehair
Moccasins	Early, side-sewn; decorated with keyhole or Blackfoot U
Associated tribes	Hidatsas (very close), Mandans, Arikaras

Western Sioux

Robe design	Feathered circle; bilaterally symmetrical
Accessories	Hair-pipe necklaces; hair-pipe breastplate

	after 1870; dentalia choker; hair tassels or feathers on garments
Beading	Lazy stitch with humped lanes
Beaded triangle	Short and wide
Other designs	Open and spreading; narrow lines common
Beads	"Cut" silver and bronze used in 1890's
Background colors	White predominately; also light blue
Cloth	Vest popular after introduction
Breechcloth	Long in back
Metal	Tinklers common in the 1880's
Hair styles	Frontal lock; long braids
Headgear	Bull tail; "sun" bonnet
Shirt	Hide shirt painted in two base colors
Dress	Three-skin with "notched" cape; fully beaded yoke, often with light-blue background
	Cloth: long gussets, square "wings"; concentric rings of dentalia common as decoration
Leggings	Bottom tabs short or absent
Moccasins	Great variety of designs
Associated tribes	Assiniboins (often used dark-blue or purple backgrounds in their beadwork); prairie tribes

Cheyennes

Robe design	Border and box; bilaterally symmetrical
Accessories	Hair tassels on garments; hair-pipe breastplate; armbands very common
Beading	Lazy stitch with flat lanes
Beaded triangle	High-stepped
Other designs	Square box common
Beads	Small 5/0 and 6/0; "cut" beads frequent
Background color	White

Cloth	Navajo blankets used; black vest a popular trade item very early; blanket often made from two pieces of strouding sewn together with the selvage forming a white line down the center
Breechcloth	Long in front and back[2]
Metal	Early use of tinklers; hair plates prominent
Hair styles	Long hair; braids often cloth-wrapped
Headgear	Roach; single feathers; "sun" bonnet; turban
Shirt	None before arrival of whites; trade shirts (solid color, pin-striped, or with designs) very popular
Dress	Early, wrap-around; later, three-skin with square-cut cape
Leggings	Women, boot moccasins; men, "forked" style
Moccasins	Attached tails; Maltese cross and longitudinal stripes common among the associated Arapahoes
Associated tribes	Arapahoes; Kiowas and Comanches (Southern Cheyennes); Western Sioux (Northern Cheyennes)

Comanches

Robe design	Border and hourglass
Accessories	Bead and shell earrings and necklaces; early use of hair-pipe chokers and breastplates; long twisted fringes; garters
Beading	Netting, loom beading or narrow lanes of lazy stitch or overlay as trim
Beaded triangle	Small wide-based
Other designs	"Leafy floral" later
Beads	Very small 4/0 and 5/0; since 1930, 12/0 and 13/0 cut Czech

Background colors	White usually; occasionally various blues
Cloth	Navajo blankets
Breechcloth	Early, ornamented with shells, and so on[3]
Metal	Early use of metals
Hair styles	Frontal lock; long
Headgear	Hair plates and beads
Shirt	None before arrival of whites; fringed at elbows
Dress	Three-skin with elaborate cutting of yoke at waist; elk-teeth decoration
Leggings	Women, boot moccasins; men, long fringes and bottom tabs
Moccasins	Long fringes; narrow lanes of beads as edging
Associated tribes	Kiowas, Cheyennes, and Arapahoes

Prairie Tribes

Robe design	Feathered circle; bilaterally symmetrical
Accessories	Early bustle; earrings frequent; hair-pipe chokers; claw necklaces very common; beaded collars and garters
Beading	Edgings; narrow lanes in overlay as trim
Beaded triangle	Uncommon
Other designs	Six-pointed star; hand
Beads	Small
Background colors	White
Cloth	Ribbon appliqué; velvet trim; some weaving
Breechcloth	Short front and back
Metal	Little used
Hair styles	Shaved — scalp lock (pigtail "horn")
Headgear	Hair bows; roaches and turbans prominent
Shirt	No shirts, but occasional cloaks and simple ponchos
Dress	Early, wrap-around; later, two-skin

Leggings	Tight below knee and cut with points projecting above front seam; bottom tab; scalp locks attached[4]
Moccasins	Edging beadwork as trim
Associated tribes	Pawnees related to village tribes; others distantly related to Sioux—transitional between Plains and Woodland tribes

APPENDICES

My hope is that the reader will use this text not as a final source of information but as a guide for further study. Some good suppliers of raw materials and of finished costume articles are given in Appendix A. Museums with outstanding collections of Plains Indian material are listed in Appendix B. The reader is also urged to consult appropriate works listed in the Bibliography.

APPENDIX A
SUPPLIERS

Museum of the American Indian, Broadway at 155th Street, New York, New York 10032 (Color slides; publications)

Walbead, Inc., 38 West 37th Street, New York, New York 10018 (Beads)

T. N. Luther, P.O. Box 6083, Shawnee Mission, Kansas 66206 (Books)

Del Trading Post, Mission, South Dakota 57555 (Miscellaneous supplies and costume pieces)

Grey Owl Indian Craft Manufacturing Company, 150-02 Beaver Road, Jamaica, New York 11433 (Supplies)

Pawnee Bill's Indian Trading Post, Pawnee, Oklahoma 74058 (Supplies, costumes)

Plume Trading and Sales Company, P.O. Box 585, Monroe, New York 10950 (Supplies)

Mrs. E. M. Roberts, 211 West Broadway, Anadarko, Oklahoma 73005 (Supplies, costumes)

M. Schwartz and Son, Inc., 321-25 East 3rd Street, New York, New York 10009 (Feathers)

Supernaw's Oklahoma Indian Supply, 301 East Rogers Boulevard, Skiatook, Oklahoma 74070 (Supplies, costumes)

Western Trading Post, 31 Broadway, Denver, Colorado 80203 (Supplies, beads)

Del Orr, 33 West Girard Avenue, Englewood, Colorado 80110 (Supplies)

Ozark Trading Post, P.O. Box 25644, Oklahoma City, Oklahoma 73125 (Supplies, beads)

Eepee Tepee Trading Company, 260 South Poteet Road, Barrington, Illinois 60010 (Supplies)

Wakeda Trading Post, Box 19146-A, Sacramento, California 95819 (Supplies)

Winona Indian Trading Post, P.O. Box 324, Santa Fe, New Mexico   87501 (Supplies, relics)

Indian Arts and Crafts Board, Room 4004, United Stated Department of the Interior, Washington, D.C. 20240. Write for their "Fact Sheet: Sources of Supply for Indian Arts and Crafts Products," a regularly updated listing of both individuals and organizations selling superior costume pieces.

APPENDIX B
MUSEUMS

American Museum of Natural History, New York City

Brooklyn Museum, Brooklyn, New York

Cleveland Museum of Natural History, Cleveland, Ohio

Denver Art Museum, Denver, Colorado

Field Museum of Natural History, Chicago, Illinois

Hudson's Bay Company Museum, Winnipeg, Manitoba

Sioux Museum, Rapid City, South Dakota

Milwaukee City Museum, Milwaukee, Wisconsin

Museum of the American Indian, New York City

Museum of Anthropology, University of California, Berkeley

Museum of the Plains Indian, Browning, Montana

Museum of the Southern Plains Indians, Anadarko, Oklahoma

Nebraska State Historical Society, Lincoln

Dress Clothing of the Plains Indians

North Dakota State Historical Society, Bismarck

University Museum, Philadelphia, Pennsylvania

National Museum of Canada, Ottawa

Neville Museum, Green Bay, Wisconsin

Oklahoma Historical Museum, Oklahoma City

Peabody Museum, Harvard University, Cambridge, Massachusetts

Southwest Museum, Los Angeles, California

United States National Museum (Smithsonian Institution), Washington, D.C.

Great Lakes Indian Museum, Cross Village, Michigan

Osage Museum, Pawhuska, Oklahoma

Fort Buford Museum, Fort Buford, North Dakota

Museum of the Fur Trade, Chadron, Nebraska

Indian City Museum, Anadarko, Oklahoma

NOTES

Chapter 1

1. Clark Wissler, "The Influence of the Horse in the Development of Plains Culture," *American Anthropologist*, n.s., Vol. XVI, No. 1 (January–March, 1914).

2. Harold E. Driver and William C. Massey, "Comparative Studies of North American Indians," American Philosophical Society *Transactions*, Vol. XLVII, Part 2 (1957), 173.

3. *Ibid.*

4. Clark Wissler, "Costumes of the Plains Indians," American Museum of Natural History *Anthropological Papers*, Vol. XVII (1915), 90.

5. Federick H. Douglas (ed.), Denver Art Museum, Department of Indian Art *Indian Leaflet Series*, No. 24, 94.

Chapter 2

1. Edwin T. Denig, "Indian Tribes of the Upper Missouri," Smithsonian Institution, Bureau of American Ethnology *Forty-sixth Annual Report, 1928–1929* (1930).

2. James Mooney, "The Ghost Dance Religion and the Sioux Outbreak of 1890," Smithsonian Institution, Bureau of American Ethnology *Fourteenth Annual Report, 1892–1893* (1896), 982.

3. Alfred L. Kroeber, "Ethnology of the Gros Ventre," American Museum of Natural History *Anthropological Papers*, Vol. I, Part 4 (1908);

Alice C. Fletcher and Francis LaFlesche, "The Omaha Tribe," Smithsonian Institution, Bureau of American Ethnology *Twenty-seventh Annual Report, 1905–1906* (1911), Plate 3.

4. Mooney, "The Ghost Dance Religion . . .," Bureau of American Ethnology *Fourteenth Annual Report, 1892–1893* (1896), 992–93.

5. Julian H. Salomon, *Book of Indian Crafts and Indian Lore*; W. Ben Hunt, *Golden Book of Indian Crafts and Lore.*

6. Kroeber, "Ethnology of the Gros Ventre," *Anthropological Papers*, Vol. I, Part 4 (1908), 268–69.

7. Letter from Charles M. Eberhart, Western Trading Post, April 17, 1963; D. G. Mandelbaum, "The Plains Cree," American Museum of Natural History *Anthropological Papers*, Vol. XXXVII (1940).

8. Garrick Mallery, "Picture-writing of the American Indians," Smithsonian Institution, Bureau of American Ethnology *Tenth Annual Report, 1888–1889* (1893), 433–37. Mallery has, in turn, quoted from Prinz Maximilian von Wied-Neuwied, *Travels in the Interior of North America*, 149, 339, 386; Mary Eastman, *Dahcotah*; George P. Belden, *Belden, the White Chief*, 277; Henry A. Boller, *Among the Indians*, 284; and James W. Lynd, "The Religion of the Dakotas," Minnesota Historical Society *Collections*, Vol. II, Part 2 (1860), 68.

9. W. J. McGee, "Ponka Feather Symbolism," *American Anthropologist*, Vol. XI (1898), 157.

10. Norman Feder, "Quill and Horsehair Feather Ornaments," *American Indian Hobbyist*, Vol. VI, Nos. 9, 10 (1960), 109.

11. Norman Feder, *Head and Tail Fans*; John F. McDermott, *Seth Eastman, Pictorial Historian of the Indian.*

12. Salomon, *Book of Indian Crafts and Indian Lore*, 62–63.

13. Norman Feder and Clyde Feltz, "Bustle Trailers," *American Indian Hobbyist*, Vol. III, Nos. 9, 10 (1957), 90–91.

14. Richard Conn, "Northern Plains Bustles," *American Indian Tradition*, Vol. VII, No. 1 (1960), 12–17.

15. Norman Feder, "Bottom Tab Leggings," *American Indian Tradition*,

Vol. VIII, No. 4 (1962), 148–59; Mari Sandoz, *Crazy Horse*; letter from F. Dennis Lessard, Del Trading Post, March 12, 1969.

Chapter 3

1. Carrie A. Lyford, *Quill and Beadwork of the Western Sioux*, 85–86.

2. Frances Densmore, "Teton Sioux Music," Smithsonian Institution, Bureau of American Ethnology *Bulletin 61* (1918), 124.

3. Roland B. Dixon, "The Color Symbolism of the Cardinal Points," *Journal of American Folklore*, Vol. XII (1899).

4. Feder, "Bottom Tab Leggings," *American Indian Tradition*, Vol. VIII, No. 4 (1962), 156.

5. John C. Ewers, *Blackfeet Crafts*.

6. Densmore, "Teton Sioux Music," Bureau of American Ethnology *Bulletin 61* (1918), 116.

7. Clark Wissler, "Material Culture of the Blackfoot Indians," American Museum of Natural History *Anthropological Papers*, Vol. V, Part 1 (1910), 133.

8. Garrick Mallery, "Pictographs of the North American Indians," Smithsonian Institution, Bureau of American Ethnology *Fourth Annual Report, 1882–83* (1886), 52.

9. Frances Densmore, "Uses of Plants by the Chippewa Indians," Smithsonian Institution, Bureau of American Ethnology *Forty-fourth Annual Report, 1926–1927* (1928).

10. Mallery, "Picture-writing of the American Indians," Bureau of American Ethnology *Tenth Annual Report, 1888–89* (1893), 221.

11. Alfred L. Kroeber, "The Arapaho," American Museum of Natural History *Bulletin*, Vol. XVIII, Part 1 (1902), 79–84.

12. Ernest Wallace and E. Adamson Hoebel, *The Comanches, Lords of the Southern Plains*.

13. John C. Ewers, *Plains Indian Painting*, 15–22, 45, Plates 15, 16.

14. Mallery, "Picture-writing of the American Indians," Bureau of American Ethnology *Tenth Annual Report, 1888–1889* (1893), 437–39.

15. Henry R. Schoolcraft, *History Respecting the History, Conditions and Prospects of the Indian Tribes of the United States.*

16. Salomon, *Book of Indian Crafts and Indian Lore*, 192–95.

17. Densmore, "Teton Sioux Music," Bureau of American Ethnology *Bulletin 61* (1918), 124, 359.

18. Kroeber, "The Arapaho," American Museum of Natural History *Bulletin*, Vol. XVIII, Part 1 (1902), 27–28.

19. Robert H. Lowie, "The Assiniboine," American Museum of Natural History *Anthropological Papers*, Vol. IV, Part 1 (1909).

20. Waldo R. Wedel, "Kansa Indians," Kansas Academy of Science *Transactions*, Vol. XLIX, No. 1 (1946); Elsie C. Parsons, "Notes on the Caddo," American Anthropological Association *Memoirs*, No. 57 (1941).

21. G. F. Will and Herbert J. Spinden, "The Mandans," Peabody Museum of American Archaeology and Ethnology *Harvard University Papers*, Vol. III, No. 4 (1906).

22. Mandelbaum, "The Plains Cree," American Museum of Natural History *Anthropological Papers*, Vol. XXXVII (1940).

Chapter 4

1. William C. Orchard, "Technique of Porcupine Quill Decoration among the North American Indians," Museum of the American Indian *Contributions*, Vol. IV, No. 1 (1916), 6.

2. Wissler, "Material Culture of the Blackfoot Indians," American Museum of Natural History *Anthropological Papers*, Vol. V, Part 1 (1910); Lyford, *Quill and Beadwork of the Western Sioux*; Ewers, *Blackfeet Crafts.*

3. Lyford, *Quill and Beadwork of the Western Sioux.*

4. Orchard, "Technique of Porcupine Quill Decoration," Museum of the American Indian *Contributions*, Vol. IV, No. 1 (1916), 16.

5. Lyford, *Quill and Beadwork of the Western Sioux.*

6. Orchard, "Technique of Porcupine Quill Decoration," Museum of the American Indian *Contributions*, Vol. IV, No. 1 (1916), 10.

7. Colin Taylor, "Plains Indians' Leggings," *English Westerner's Brand Book*, Vol. III, No. 2 (1961), 7.

8. Letter from Benson Lee Lanford, November 12, 1969.

Chapter 5

1. John C. Ewers, "Hair Pipes in Plains Indian Adornment," Smithsonian Institution, Bureau of American Ethnology *Bulletin* 164 (1957).

2. Ewers, *Blackfeet Crafts*; Meriwether Lewis and William Clark (ed. by Nicholas Biddle), *The Journals of the Expedition under the Command of Captains Lewis and Clark*, II, 260.

3. See Michael S. Tucker, *Old Time Sioux Dancers*.

4. Wied-Neuwied, *Travels in the Interior of North America*; Edward S. Curtis, *The North American Indian*, IV; Cohoe, *A Cheyenne Sketchbook*.

5. D. I. Bushnell, "The Various Uses of Buffalo Hair by the North American Indians," *American Anthropologist*, n.s., Vol. XI (1909), 413–23.

6. Norman Feder and Milford G. Chandler, "Grizzly Claw Necklaces," *American Indian Tradition*, Vol. VIII, No. 1 (1961), 7–16.

7. Curtis, *The North American Indian*, IV.

8. *Ibid.*; Will and Spinden, "The Mandans," Peabody Museum *Harvard University Papers*, Vol. III, No. 4 (1906); Frederick W. Hodge (ed.), "Handbook of American Indians," Smithsonian Institution, Bureau of American Ethnology *Bulletin 30*, Vol. I (1907), 17.

9. Curtis, *The North American Indian*, IV; W. Raymond Wood, "Perforated Elk Teeth: A Functional and Historical Analysis," *American Antiquity*, Vol. XXII (1957), 382.

10. Alexander Henry and David Thompson (ed. by Elliott Coues), *New Light on the Early History of the Greater Northwest*, 753; Ewers, "Hair Pipes in Plains Indian Adornment," Bureau of Ethnology *Bulletin 164* (1957); letter from B. L. Lanford, November 12, 1969.

11. Rowena W. Thorp, "The Dress of the Plains Indian Women and Children" (Master's thesis, Southern Methodist University, 1935); Mildred Mayhall, *The Kiowas*; William S. Prettyman and Robert E. Cunningham, *Indian Territory*; Curtis, *The North American Indians*, V.

12. Ewers, *Blackfeet Crafts*, 32; Will and Spinden, "The Mandans," Peabody Museum *Harvard University Papers*, Vol. III, No. 4 (1906); letter from

Mrs. F. Dennis (Rosemary) Lessard, May 6, 1965; Richard Conn, "Cheyenne Style Beadwork," *American Indian Tradition*, Vol. VII, No. 2 (1961), 47.

13. Kroeber, "Ethnology of the Gros Ventre," American Museum of Natural History *Anthropological Papers*, Vol. I, Part 4 (1908), 275; McDermott, *Seth Eastman, Pictorial Historian of the Indian*; Hodge, "Handbook of American Indians," Bureau of American Ethnology *Bulletin 30* (1930) I.

14. Kroeber, "The Arapaho," American Museum of Natural History *Bulletin*, Vol. XVIII, Part 1 (1902), 150.

15. Mandelbaum, "The Plains Cree," American Museum of Natural History *Anthropological Papers*, Vol. XXXVII (1940).

Chapter 6

1. Driver and Massey, "Comparative Studies of North American Indians," American Philosophical Society *Transactions*, n.s., Vol. XLVII, Part 2 (1957), 378; Joseph Jablow, "The Cheyenne in Plains Indian Trade Relations (1795–1840)," American Ethnological Society *Monographs*, No. 19 (1951).

2. Values of goods are given by Denig, "Indian Tribes of the Upper Missouri," Bureau of American Ethnology *Forty-sixth Annual Report, 1928–1929* (1930), 585–88. See also Fletcher and LaFlesche, "The Omaha Tribe," Bureau of American Ethnology *Twenty-seventh Annual Report, 1905–1906* (1911), 611–22.

3. William C. Orchard, "Beads and Beadwork of the American Indians," Museum of the American Indian *Contributions*, Vol. XI (1929), 13.

4. Arthur Woodward, *Indian Trade Goods*.

5. Lewis and Clark, *Journals*; George Catlin, *Letters and Notes on the Manners, Customs and Conditions of the North American Indians, Written During Eight Years Travel, 1832–39*; George Bird Grinnell, *The Cheyenne Indians, Their History and Ways of Life*; Orchard, "Beads and Beadwork of the American Indian," Museum of the American Indian *Contributions*, Vol. XI (1929), 78–81.

6. Woodward, *Indian Trade Goods*.

7. For further information on bead types, see Woodward, *Indian Trade*

Goods; on fancy beads, Orchard, "Beads and Beadwork," cited above; on the history of beadwork, Ewers, *Blackfeet Crafts,* and Lyford, *Quill and Beadwork of the Western Sioux.*

8. Milford G. Chandler and David A. Kracinski, "Unusual Beadwork Techniques, Part I," *American Indian Tradition,* Vol. VIII, No. 5 (1962), 200; Orchard, "Beads and Beadwork of the American Indian," Museum of the American Indian *Contributions,* Vol. XI (1929), 5.

9. David A. Kracinski, "Unusual Beadwork Techniques, Part II," *American Indian Tradition,* Vol. IX, No. 1 (1963), 38.

10. E. LaQuay, "Beadwork," *Powwow Trails,* Vol. I, No. 6 (1964); Conn, "Cheyenne Style Beadwork," *American Indian Tradition,* Vol. VII, No. 2 (1961), 48, 51.

11. Douglas, Denver Art Museum, Department of Indian Art *Indian Leaflet Series,* No. 73–74, 92; *ibid.,* No. 117, 66–68.

12. Douglas, Denver Art Museum, Department of Indian Art *Indian Leaflet Series,* No. 117, 66–68.

13. Lyford, *Quill and Beadwork of the Western Sioux,* 71.

14. Conn, "Cheyenne Style Beadwork," *American Indian Tradition,* Vol. VII, No. 2 (1961); for a good comparison, see Douglas, Denver Art Museum, Department of Indian Art *Indian Leaflet Series,* No. 73–74, 89; Tables 2 and 3 are based on Louis H. Powell, "A Study of Indian Beadwork of the North Central Plains," St. Paul Science Museum *Indian Leaflets,* Nos. 5–7 (1953), supplemented with information from many other sources.

15. William Wildschut and John E. Ewers, "Crow Indian Beadwork," Museum of the American Indian *Contributions,* Vol. XVI (1959), 45; O. R. Gallagher and L. H. Powell, "Time Perspective in Plains Indian Beaded Art," *American Anthropologist,* n.s., Vol. LV (1953), 610; Richard Conn, "Western Sioux Beadwork," *American Indian Hobbyist,* Vol. VI, Nos. 9, 10 (1960), 118; Tucker, *Old Time Sioux Dancers;* Powell, "A Study of Indian Beadwork," St. Paul Science Museum *Indian Leaflets,* Nos. 5–7 (1953); Robert Ridgway, *Color Standards and Color Nomenclature,* a text consisting primarily of a series of color "chips."

16. Gallagher and Powell, "Time Perspective in Plains Indian Beaded Art," *American Anthropologist,* n.s., Vol. LV (1953), 612.

17. Powell, "A Study of Indian Beadwork," St. Paul Science Museum *Indian Leaflets,* Nos. 5–7 (1953).

18. John C. Ewers, "Three Ornaments Worn by Upper Missouri Indians a Century and a Quarter Ago," New York Historical Society *Quarterly*, Vol. XLI (1957), 28–29.

19. Donn Charnley, "Crow Loop Necklace," *American Indian Hobbyist*, Vol. V, Nos. 5, 6 (1959), 60–62.

Chapter 7

1. Norman Feder, "Plains Indian Metalworking," *American Indian Tradition*, Vol. VIII, Nos. 2, 3 (1962).

2. Donald Jackson (ed.), *Letters of the Lewis and Clark Expedition.* The *Journals* themselves add bells (probably "hawk"), brass wire, moccasins, and "looking glasses" to this list.

3. Feder, "Plains Indian Metalworking," *American Indian Tradition*, Vol. VIII, Nos. 2, 3 (1962).

4. *Ibid.*

5. Letter from F. Dennis Lessard, October 2, 1964.

6. Robert H. Lowie, "Crow Indian Art," American Museum of Natural History *Anthropological Papers*, Vol. XXI, Part 4 (1922); Kroeber, "Ethnology of the Gros Ventre," American Museum of Natural History *Anthropological Papers*, Vol. I, Part 4 (1908); Lyford, *Quill and Beadwork of the Western Sioux*, 25; Gallagher and Powell, "Time Perspective in Plains Indian Beaded Art," *American Anthropologist*, n.s., Vol. LV (1953), 612.

7. Margo Jester, "Peace Medals," *American Indian Tradition*, Vol. VII, No. 5 (1961); Kenneth M. Failor and Eleonora Hayden, *Medals of the United States Mint*, 267.

8. Norman Feder and Clyde Feltz, "Old Time Sioux Costume," *American Indian Hobbyist*, Vol. IV, Nos. 3, 4 (1957), 29.

9. Arthur Woodward, *Indian Trade Goods*; Stanley J. Olsen, "Dating Early Plains Buttons by Their Form," *American Antiquity*, Vol. XXVIII, No. 4 (1963), 553.

10. Feder, "Plains Indian Metalworking," *American Indian Tradition*, Vol. VIII, Nos. 2, 3 (1962), 103.

11. *Ibid.*, 73.

12. Wissler, "Material Culture of the Blackfoot Indians," American Mu-

seum of Natural History *Anthropological Papers*, Vol. V, Part 1 (1910).

13. Norman Feder and Clyde Feltz, "Modern Plateau Dance Costume," *American Indian Hobbyist*, Vol. III, Nos. 9, 10 (1957).

Chapter 8

1. Letter from Benson Lee Lanford, November 12, 1969.

2. Cohoe, *A Cheyenne Sketchbook*.

3. Ewers, *Blackfeet Crafts*.

4. Letter from Rosemary Lessard, March 12, 1969.

5. Bill Holm, "Making a Blanket 'Capote'," *American Indian Hobbyist*, Vol. III, No. 1 (1956).

6. Wildschut and Ewers, "Crow Indian Beadwork," Museum of the American Indian *Contributions*, Vol. XVI (1959), Fig. 10.

7. Holm, "Making a Blanket 'Capote'," *American Indian Hobbyist*, Vol. III, No. 1 (1956).

8. Curtis, in *The North American Indian*, IV, 23, said the Crows were late in adopting the breechcloth.

9. Bill Holm in Norman Feder, "The Crow Indians of Montana," *American Indian Hobbyist*, Vol. V, Nos. 5, 6 (1959); Prettyman and Cunningham, *Indian Territory*; Wissler, "Material Culture of the Blackfoot Indians," American Museum of Natural History *Anthropological Papers*, Vol. V, Part 1 (1910), 119; Cohoe, *A Cheyenne Sketchbook*; conversation with Frederick J. Dockstader, November 1, 1963.

10. Holm in Feder, "The Crow Indians of Montana," *American Indian Hobbyist*, Vol. V, Nos. 5, 6 (1959).

11. Richard Conn, "Blackfeet Women's Clothing," *American Indian Tradition*, Vol. VII, No. 4 (1961), 124–25.

12. Wissler, "Material Culture of the Blackfoot Indians," American Museum of Natural History *Anthropological Papers*, Vol. V, Part 1 (1910), 126.

13. Richard Conn, "Braided Sashes," *American Indian Tradition*, Vol. IX, No. 1 (1963).

14. Grace G. Denny, *Fabrics*.

15. Colin Taylor, "The Plains Indian Shirt," *American Indian Tradition,* Vol. III, Nos. 7, 8 (1957), 65.

16. Alice Marriott, "Ribbon Applique Work of North American Indians, Part I," Oklahoma Anthropological Society *Bulletin,* Vol. VI (March, 1958); Norman Feder, "Ribbon Applique," *American Indian Hobbyist,* Vol. III, Nos. 2, 3 (1956).

Chapter 9

1. Clark Wissler, *North American Indians of the Plains.*

2. Curtis, *The North American Indian.*

3. Hodge, "Handbook of American Indians," Bureau of American Ethnology *Bulletin 30,* Vol. I (1907), 524.

4. Will and Spinden, "The Mandans," Peabody Museum *Harvard University Papers,* Vol. III, No. 4 (1906).

5. Wissler, "Material Culture of the Blackfoot Indians," American Museum of Natural History *Anthropological Papers,* Vol. V, Part 1 (1910), 131.

6. Kroeber, "Ethnology of the Gros Ventre," American Museum of Natural History *Anthropological Papers,* Vol. I, Part 4 (1908), 273; for a good illustration, see Bear Bull in Ralph W. Andrews, *Curtis' Western Indians,* 123.

7. Wissler, "Material Culture of the Blackfoot Indians," American Museum of Natural History *Anthropological Papers,* Vol. V, Part 1 (1910), 132.

8. Curtis, *The North American Indian;* Ellsworth Jaeger, *Wildwood Wisdom,* 296–99.

9. Frances Densmore, in "Teton Sioux Music," Bureau of American Ethnology *Bulletin 61* (1918), 360, disputes use among the Western Sioux. Construction of a Blackfoot specimen has been described by William Guy Spittal in "Blackfeet Hair Ornament," *American Indian Hobbyist,* Vol. II, No. 8 (1956).

10. Kroeber, "The Arapaho," American Museum of Natural History *Bulletin,* Vol. XVIII, Part 1 (1902), 55.

11. Norman Feder, "Plains Hair and Roach Ornaments," *American Indian Hobbyist,* Vol. IV, Nos. 9, 10 (1958); Wissler, "Material Culture of the

Blackfoot Indians," American Museum of Natural History *Anthropological Papers*, Vol. V, Part 1 (1910), 152.

12. Ewers, "Hair Pipes in Plains Indian Adornment," Bureau of American Ethnology *Bulletin 164* (1957), Plate 6; Bill Holm in Feder, "The Crow Indians of Montana," *American Indian Tradition*, Vol. V, Nos. 5, 6 (1959).

13. Cohoe, *A Cheyenne Sketchbook*.

14. Kroeber, "The Arapaho," American Museum of Natural History *Bulletin*, Vol. XVIII, Part 1 (1902), 52; Kroeber, "Ethnology of the Gros Ventre," American Museum of Natural History *Anthropological Papers*, Vol. I, Part 4 (1908), 269.

15. Mandelbaum, "The Plains Cree," American Museum of Natural History *Anthropological Papers*, Vol. XXXVII (1940), 208–209.

16. Lowie, "The Assiniboine," American Museum of Natural History *Anthropological Papers*, Vol. IV, Part 1 (1909); Alexander Ross, *The Fur Hunters of the Far West*, I, 306.

17. Norman Feder, "Otter Fur Turbans," *American Indian Tradition*, Vol. VII, No. 3 (1961).

18. George Catlin, *Letters and Notes on the Manners, Customs and Conditions of the North American Indians*, II, 23; Wallace and Hoebel, *The Comanches, Lords of the Southern Plains*.

19. Catlin, *Letters and Notes on . . . North American Indians*, II, 23–24.

20. James H. Howard, "The Roach Headdress," *American Indian Hobbyist*, Vol. VI, Nos. 7, 8 (1960).

21. Letter from Charles M. Eberhart, Western Trading Post, April 17, 1963.

22. Wissler, "Material Culture of the Blackfoot Indians," American Museum of Natural History *Anthropological Papers*, Vol. V, Part 1 (1910); Michael G. Johnson, "Blackfeet Bonnet," *Powwow Trails*, Vol. II, No. 5 (1965).

23. William P. Clark, *The Indian Sign Language with Brief Explanatory Notes . . .* , 398.

24. Mandelbaum, "The Plains Cree," American Museum of Natural History *Anthropological Papers*, Vol. XXXVII (1940), 208–209.

25. Douglas, Denver Art Museum, Department of Indian Art *Indian Leaf-*

let Series, No. 24. Details of the construction of such bonnets are given by William Guy Spittal, "Blackfeet Horned Headdress," *American Indian Hobbyist*, Vol. II, No. 8 (1956), and by Norman Feder, "Shoshone Split-Horn Bonnet," *American Indian Hobbyist*, Vol. VI, Nos. 3, 4 (1959), for the Shoshonis.

26. Kroeber, "The Arapaho," American Museum of Natural History *Bulletin*, Vol. XVIII, Part 1 (1902), 136–37.

27. Lowie, "The Assiniboine," American Museum of Natural History *Anthropological Papers*, Vol. IV, Part 1 (1909), 65–66.

28. Herbert J. Spinden, "The Nez Percé Indians," American Anthropological Association *Memoirs*, Vol. II (1908), 191–93, 220.

Chapter 10

1. Ewers, *Blackfeet Crafts*.
2. Hodge, "Handbook of American Indians," Bureau of American Ethnology *Bulletin 30* (1907), II, 591–94.
3. Taylor, "Plains Indians' Leggings," *English Westerner's Brand Book*, Vol. III, No. 2 (1961), 3.
4. Wildschut and Ewers, "Crow Indian Beadwork," Museum of the American Indian *Contributions*, Vol. XVI (1959), 19.
5. Kaj Birket-Smith, "Contributions to the Ethnology of the Chipewyan," *Report of the Fifth Thule Expedition*, Vol. V, No. 3 (1930), 52; Kroeber, "The Arapaho," American Museum of Natural History *Bulletin*, Vol. XVIII, Part 1 (1902), Plate 35; Francis LaFlesche, "The Osage Tribe," Smithsonian Institution, Bureau of American Ethnology *Thirty-sixth Annual Report, 1914–1915* (1921), Plate 11.
6. For definitions and distributions of these hide articles, the author is indebted to Richard G. Conn, "A Classification of Aboriginal North American Clothing" (Master's thesis, University of Washington, 1955).
7. Wissler, "Costumes of the Plains Indians," American Museum of Natural History *Anthropological Papers*, Vol. XVII (1915), Figure 12; Michael G. Johnson, "A Note on Indian Coats and Jackets," *Powwow Trails*, Vol. V, No. 8 (1969).
8. Will and Spinden, "The Mandans," Peabody Museum *Harvard University Papers*, Vol. III, No. 4 (1906).

9. Taylor, "The Plains Indian Shirt," *American Indian Hobbyist,* Vol. III, Nos. 7, 8 (1957).

10. *Ibid.*

11. Spinden, "The Nez Perce Indians," American Anthropological Association *Memoirs,* Vol. II (1908), 217; Herbert W. Krieger, "American Indian Costumes in the United States National Museum," Smithsonian Institution *Annual Report for 1928* (1929).

12. Wied-Neuwied, *Travels in the Interior of North America.*

13. Julian H. Salomon, *The Book of Indian Crafts and Indian Lore,* 71–72.

14. Curtis, *The North American Indian,* III, 30.

15. Letter from Charles M. Eberhart, April 17, 1963.

16. Prettyman and Cunningham, *Indian Territory.*

17. Conn, "A Classification of Aboriginal North American Clothing (Master's thesis, University of Washington, 1955), 37; Wildschut and Ewers, "Crow Indian Beadwork," Museum of the American Indian *Contributions,* Vol. XVI (1959), 11.

Chapter 11

1. Conn, "A Classification of Aboriginal North American Clothing," (Master's thesis, University of Washington, 1955).

2. Rosemary Lessard, in a letter dated April 24, 1965, thinks Conn misinterpreted the data on the "one-sleeve" dress. She says he had the side-fold or side-seam dress in mind.

3. Letter from R. Lessard, March 12, 1969.

4. Wissler, "Material Culture of the Blackfoot Indians," American Museum of Natural History *Anthropological Papers,* Vol. V, Part 1 (1910), 138–39.

5. Shan Little, "A Sioux Woman's Dentalium Shell Dress," *American Indian Crafts and Culture,* Vol. II, No. 10 (1968).

Chapter 12

1. Douglas, Denver Art Museum, Department of Indian Art *Indian Leaflet Series,* No. 24, 95.

2. Conn, "A Classification of Aboriginal North American Clothing" (Master's thesis, University of Washington, 1955), 29, and Table 11; Norman Feder, "Front Seam Leggings," *American Indian Tradition*, Vol. VIII, No. 3 (1962); Paul Radin, "The Winnebago Tribe," Smithsonian Institution, Bureau of American Ethnology *Thirty-seventh Annual Report, 1915–1916* (1923), 106.

3. Taylor, "Plains Indians' Leggings," *English Westerner's Brand Book*, Vol. III, No. 2 (1961), 3.

4. Feder, "Bottom Tab Leggings," *American Indian Tradition*, Vol. VIII, No. 4 (1962), 158.

5. W. C. Farabee, "Dress Among Plains Indian Women," University of Pennsylvania Museum *Journal*, Vol. XII (1921).

6. Dennis Evans, "Southern Plains Women's Boots," *American Indian Tradition*, Vol. VIII, No. 5 (1962).

7. Douglas, Denver Art Museum, Department of Indian Art *Indian Leaflet Series*, No. 24. 96.

8. Conn, "A Classification of Aboriginal North American Clothing" (Master's thesis, University of Washington, 1955), 18.

9. Feder, "Bottom Tab Leggings," *American Indian Tradition*, Vol. VIII, No. 4 (1962), 159.

10. Michael G. Johnson, "Indian Beadwork from the Canadian Plains," *Powwow Trails*, Vol. V, No. 10 (1969); *ibid.*, "Western Sioux Man's Costume 1880–1910," *Powwow Trails*, Vol. VI, Nos. 1, 2 (1969).

Chapter 13

1. Wildschut and Ewers, "Crow Indian Beadwork," Museum of the American Indian *Contributions*, Vol. XVI (1959), 21; Clark, *The Indian Sign Language with Brief Explanatory Notes . . .*; Wissler, "Material Culture of the Blackfoot Indians," American Museum of Natural History *Anthropological Papers*, Vol. V, Part 1 (1910). The author added Crows to Wissler's list.

2. Salomon, *Book of Indian Crafts and Indian Lore*, 93.

3. Wissler, "Material Culture of the Blackfoot Indians," American Museum of Natural History *Anthropological Papers*, Vol. V, Part 1 (1910), 151.

4. Letter from Rosemary Lessard, March 12, 1969.

5. Wallace and Hoebel, *The Comanches, Lords of the Southern Plains.*

6. Mandelbaum, "The Plains Cree," American Museum of Natural History *Anthropological Papers,* Vol. XXXVII (1940).

7. Clark Wissler, "Distribution of Moccasin Decorations among the Plains Tribes," American Museum of Natural History *Anthropological Papers,* Vol. XXIX, Part 1 (1927).

8. *Ibid.,* 19–20.

9. Kroeber, "Ethnology of the Gros Ventre," American Museum of Natural History *Anthropological Papers,* Vol. I, Part 4 (1908), 156–60; Feder, "The Crow Indians of Montana," *American Indian Tradition,* Vol. V, Nos. 5, 6 (1959); Wissler, "Distribution of Moccasin Decorations," American Museum of Natural History *Anthropological Papers,* Vol. XXIX, Part 1 (1927), 19.

Chapter 14

1. Douglas, Denver Art Museum, Department of Indian Art *Indian Leaflet Series,* No. 24, 96.

2. Clark Wissler, "Societies and Ceremonial Associations in the Oglala Division of the Teton-Dakota," American Museum of Natural History *Anthropological Papers,* Vol. XI, Part 1 (1912), 95.

3. Driver and Massey, "Comparative Studies of North American Indians," American Philosophical Society *Transactions,* n.s., Vol. XLVII, Part 2 (1957), 254–55; see also A. Irving Hallowell, "Bear Ceremonialism in the Northern Hemisphere," *American Anthropologist,* n.s., Vol. XXVIII, No. 1 (1926).

4. Based on Densmore, "Teton Sioux Music," Bureau of American Ethnology *Bulletin 61* (1918), 314ff.

5. Robert H. Lowie, "Societies of the Crow, Hidatsa and Mandan Indians," American Museum of Natural History *Anthropological Papers,* Vol. XI, Part 3 (1913).

6. Wissler, "Societies and Ceremonial Associations," American Museum of Natural History *Anthropological Papers,* Vol. XI, Part 1 (1912), 37–38.

7. Mooney, "The Ghost Dance Religion and the Sioux Outbreak of

1890," Bureau of American Ethnology *Fourteenth Annual Report, 1892–1893* (1896), 798, 823.

8. Clark Wissler, "General Discussion of Shamanistic and Dancing Societies," American Museum of Natural History *Anthropological Papers*, Vol. XI, Part 12 (1916).

9. For additional information on the crow belt, see Fletcher and La-Flesche, "The Omaha Tribe," Bureau of American Ethnology *Twenty-seventh Annual Report, 1905–1906* (1911), 441–46.

10. Based on James H. Howard, "Northern Plains Grass Dance Costume," *American Indian Tradition*, Vol. VII, No. 1 (1960).

11. Jerry Smith, "Otter Drop," *American Indian Crafts and Culture*, Vol. II, No. 4 (1968).

12. Robert Austin, "Fingerweaving," *Powwow Trails*, Vol. VI, No. 7 (1969).

13. Based on Jerry Smith, "Oklahoma Straight Dancer," paper written for the California Indian Hobbyist Association ca. 1968; see also James H. Howard and Gertrude P. Kurath, "Ponca Dances, Ceremonies and Music," *Ethnomusicology*, Vol. II (1959).

14. Based on Norman Feder, "Oklahoma Fancy Dance Costume," *American Indian Hobbyist*, Vol. IV, Nos. 5, 6 (1958); William K. Powers, *Grass Dance Costume*; ibid., "Feathers Costume," *Powwow Trails*, Vol. III, Nos. 7, 8 (1966); Jerry Smith, *Oklahoma Fancy Dance Outfit*; Jerry Smith and Randy Kroha, "Oklahoma Fancy Dancers, 1972," *American Indian Crafts and Culture*, Vol. VI, No. 5 (1972); and Tyrone H. Stewart and Jerry Smith, *The Oklahoma Feather Dancer*.

15. James H. Howard, "Pan-Indian Culture of Oklahoma," *Scientific Monthly*, Vol. LXXXI (November, 1955), 215–20.

16. Driver and Massey, "Comparative Studies of North American Indians," American Philosophical Society *Transactions*, n.s., Vol. XLVII, Part 2 (1957), 271.

Chapter 15

1. Wissler, "Material Culture of the Blackfoot Indians," American Museum of Natural History *Anthropological Papers*, Vol. V, Part 1 (1910), 123.

2. Cohoe, *A Cheyenne Sketchbook*, 30.

3. Thomas Donaldson, "The George Catlin Indian Gallery in the United States National Museum," Smithsonian Institution *Annual Report for 1885* (1887), 49.

4. Cohoe, *A Cheyenne Sketchbook*, 69.

BIBLIOGRAPHY

Books, General

Appleton, Leroy H. *Indian Art of the Americas.* New York, Scribner, 1950.

Clark, William P. *The Indian Sign Language with Brief Explanatory Notes.* . . . Philadelphia, L. R. Hamersly, 1885.

Cohoe. *A Cheyenne Sketchbook.* Norman, University of Oklahoma Press, 1964.

Denny, Grace G. *Fabrics.* Philadelphia, Lippincott, 1947.

Eastman, Mary. *Dahcotah.* New York, J. Wiley, 1849.

Ewers, John C. *Plains Indian Painting.* Palo Alto, California, Stanford University, 1939.

Gregg, Josiah. *Commerce of the Prairies.* Ed. by Max L. Moorhead. Norman, University of Oklahoma Press, 1954.

Grinnell, George Bird. *The Cheyenne Indians, Their History and Ways of Life.* 2 vols. New Haven and London, Yale University Press, 1923.

Haines, Francis. *The Buffalo.* New York, Crowell, 1970.

Hoebel, E. Adamson. *The Cheyennes.* New York, Holt, Rinehart and Winston, 1960.

Hyde, George E. *Pawnee Indians.* Denver, University of Denver, 1951; new edition, Norman, University of Oklahoma Press, 1974.

Jackson, Donald, ed. *Letters of the Lewis and Clark Expedition.* Urbana, University of Illinois, 1962.

Jacobson, Oscar B. *North American Indian Costumes.* Nice, France, C. Szwedzicki, 1952.

Jaeger, Ellsworth. *Wildwood Wisdom.* New York, Macmillan, 1945.

Josephy, Alvin M., Jr., ed. *The American Heritage Book of Indians.* New York, Simon and Schuster, 1961.

LaFarge, Oliver. *Pictorial History of the American Indian.* New York, Crown, 1957.

Long, James Larpenteur (First Boy). *The Assiniboines.* Ed. by Michael S. Kennedy. Norman, University of Oklahoma Press, 1961.

Lowie, Robert H. *The Crow Indians.* New York, Farrar and Rinehart, 1935.

———. *Indians of the Plains.* Garden City, Natural History Press, 1963.

Mason, Bernard S. *Dances and Stories of the American Indian.* New York, Barnes, 1944.

Mayhall, Mildred. *The Kiowas.* Norman, University of Oklahoma Press, 1962.

McKenney, Thomas L., and James Hall. *Indian Tribes of North America.* Edinburgh, John Grant, 1933.

Morgan, Lewis Henry. *The Indian Journals, 1859–1862.* Ed. by Leslie A. White. Ann Arbor, University of Michigan, 1959.

Ridgway, Robert. *Color Standards and Color Nomenclature.* Washington, D.C., privately printed, 1912.

Salomon, Julian H. *Book of Indian Crafts and Indian Lore.* New York, Harper, 1928.

Sandoz, Mari. *Crazy Horse.* New York, Hastings, 1955.

Schoolcraft, Henry R. *History Respecting the History, Conditions and Prospects of the Indian Tribes of the United States.* Philadelphia, Lippincott, Grambo and Company, 1847.

Stirling, Matthew W., ed. *Indians of the Americas.* Washington, National Geographic Society, 1955.

Underhill, Ruth M. *Red Man's America.* Chicago, University of Chicago, 1953.

Wallace, Ernest, and E. Adamson Hoebel. *The Comanches, Lords of the Southern Plains.* Norman, University of Oklahoma Press, 1952.

Books by and About Explorers, Artists, and Photographers

Andrews, Ralph W. *Curtis' Western Indians.* Seattle, Superior Publishing Company, 1962.

———. *Indians as the Westerners Saw Them.* Seattle, Superior Publishing Company, 1963.

Belden, George P. *Belden, the White Chief, or Twelve Years among the Wild Indians of the Plains.* New York, C. F. Vent, 1870.

Boller, Henry A. *Among the Indians.* Philadelphia, T. E. Zell, 1868.

Brown, Mark H., and W. R. Felton. *The Frontier Years . . . L. A. Hoffman: Photographer of the Plains.* New York, Bramhall House, 1955.

Catlin, George. *Letters and Notes on the Manners, Customs and Conditions of the North American Indians, Written During Eight Years Travel, 1832–39.* 2 vols. New York, Wiley and Putnam, 1841.

Curtis, Edward S. *The North American Indian.* Norwood, Connecticut, privately printed, 1903–1920.

Ewers, John C. *Artists of the Old West.* Garden City, Doubleday, 1965.

Henry, Alexander, and David Thompson. *New Light on the Early History of the Greater Northwest.* Ed. by Elliott Coues. New York, Harper, 1897.

Lewis, Meriwether, and William Clark. *The Journals of the Expedition under the Command of Captains Lewis and Clark.* Ed. by Nicholas Biddle. Reprint, New York, Heritage Press, 1962.

McCracken, Harold. *George Catlin and the Old Frontier.* New York, Dial Press, 1959.

McDermott, John F. *Seth Eastman, Pictorial Historian of the Indian.* Norman, University of Oklahoma Press, 1961.

Miller, Alfred Jacob. *The West of Alfred Jacob Miller (1837). From the Notes and Watercolors in the Walters Art Gallery, with an Account of the Artist by Marvin C. Ross.* Norman, University of Oklahoma Press, 1951.

Prettyman, William S., and Robert E. Cunninhgam. *Indian Territory.* Norman, University of Oklahoma Press, 1957.

Quimby, George I. *Indians of the Western Frontier: Paintings of George Catlin.* Chicago, Chicago Natural History Museum, 1958.

Ross, Alexander. *The Fur Hunters of the Far West.* London, Smith, Elder and Company, 1855.

Schmitt, Martin F., and Dee Brown. *Fighting Indians of the West.* New York, Scribner, 1948.

Wied-Neuwied, Prinz Alexander Philip Maximilian von. *Travels in the Interior of North America.* Translated by H. Evans Lloyd. London, Ackermann and Company, 1843.

Government Publications

Note: Published in Washington by the Government Printing Office unless otherwise noted.

Denig, Edwin T. "Indian Tribes of the Upper Missouri," Smithsonian Institution, Bureau of American Ethnology *Forty-sixth Annual Report, 1928–1929.* 1930.

Densmore, Frances. "Teton Sioux Music," Smithsonian Institution, Bureau of American Ethnology *Bulletin 61.* 1918.

———. "Uses of Plants by the Chippewa Indians," Smithsonian Institution, Bureau of American Ethnology *Forty-fourth Annual Report, 1926–1927.* 1928.

Donaldson, Thomas. "The George Catlin Indian Gallery in the United States National Museum," Smithsonian Institution *Annual Report for 1885.* 1887.

Ewers, John C. *Blackfeet Crafts.* Lawrence, Kansas, Bureau of Indian Affairs, 1945.

———. "Hair Pipes in Plains Indian Adornment," Smithsonian Institution, Bureau of American Ethnology *Bulletin 164.* 1957.

———. "Selected References on the Plains Indians," Smithsonian Institution *Anthropological Bibliography 1.* 1960.

Failor, Kenneth M., and Eleonora Hayden. *Medals of the United States Mint.* 1974.

Fletcher, Alice C., and Francis LaFlesche. "The Omaha Tribe," Smithsonian Institution, Bureau of American Ethnology *Twenty-seventh Annual Report, 1905–1906.* 1911.

Hodge, Frederick W., ed. "Handbook of American Indians," Smithsonian Institution, Bureau of American Ethnology *Bulletin 30.* 1907.

Krieger, Herbert W. "American Indian Costumes in the United States National Museum," Smithsonian Institution *Annual Report for 1928.* 1929.

Kurz, Rudolph Friederich. "Journal of Rudolph Friederich Kurz," Smithsonian Institution, Bureau of American Ethnology *Bulletin 115.* Translated by Myrtis Jarrell, ed. by J. N. B. Hewitt. 1937.

LaFlesche, Francis. "The Osage Tribe: Rite of the Chiefs; Sayings of the Ancient Men," Smithsonian Institution, Bureau of American Ethnology *Thirty-sixth Annual Report, 1914–1915.* 1921.

Lyford, Carrie A. *Quill and Beadwork of the Western Sioux.* Lawrence, Kansas, Bureau of Indian Affairs, 1940.

Mallery, Garrick. "Pictographs of the North American Indians: a Preliminary Paper," Smithsonian Institution, Bureau of American Ethnology *Fourth Annual Report, 1882–1883.* 1886.

———. "Picture-writing of the American Indians," Smithsonian Institution, Bureau of American Ethnology *Tenth Annual Report, 1888–1889.* 1893.

Mooney, James. "The Ghost Dance Religion and the Sioux Outbreak of 1890," Smithsonian Institution, Bureau of American Ethnology *Fourteenth Annual Report, 1892–1893.* 1896.

Radin, Paul. "The Winnebago Tribe," Smithsonian Institution, Bureau of American Ethnology *Thirty-seventh Annual Report, 1915–1916.* 1923.

Shimkin, D. B., and Fred W. Voget. "The Wind River Shoshone Sun Dance," Smithsonian Institution, Bureau of American Ethnology *Bulletin 151.* 1953.

Swanton, John R. "Indian Tribes of North America," Smithsonian Institution, Bureau of American Ethnology *Bulletin 145.* 1953.

Journals, Monographs, Museum Bulletins, and Leaflets

Birket-Smith, Kaj. "Contributions to the Ethnology of the Chipewyan," *Report of the Fifth Thule Expedition,* Vol. V, No. 3 (1930).

Bushnell, D. I. "The Various Uses of Buffalo Hair by the North American Indians," *American Anthropologist*, n.s., Vol. XI (1909).

Dixon, Roland B. "The Color Symbolism of the Cardinal Points," *Journal of American Folk-Lore*, Vol. XII (1899).

Dorsey, George H. "The Arapaho Sun Dance," Field Museum *Anthropological Series*, Vol. 4. 1903.

———. "The Ponca Sun Dance," Field Museum *Anthropological Series*, Vol. VII. 1905.

———. "The Cheyenne," Field Museum *Anthropological Series*, Vol. IX. 1905.

Douglas, Frederick H., ed. Denver Art Museum, Department of Indian Art *Indian Leaflet Series*, 1930–53.

Driver, Harold E., and William C. Massey. "Comparative Studies of North American Indians," American Philosophical Society *Transactions*, n.s., Vol. XLVII, Part 2 (1957).

Ewers, John C. "Three Ornaments Worn by Upper Missouri Indians a Century and a Quarter Ago," New York Historical Society *Quarterly*, Vol. LXI (1957).

Farabee, W. C. "Dress Among Plains Indian Women," University of Pennsylvania Museum *Journal*, Vol. XII (1921).

Fletcher, Alice C. "Glimpses of Child-Life among the Omaha Tribe of Indian," *Journal of American Folklore*, Vol. I (1888).

Gallagher, O. R., and L. H. Powell. "Time Perspective in Plains Indian Beaded Art," *American Anthropologist*, n.s., Vol. LV (1953).

Hallowell, A. Irving. "Bear Ceremonialism in the Northern Hemisphere," *American Anthropologist*, n.s., Vol. XXVIII, No. 1 (1926).

Holmes, William H. "Areas of American Culture Characterization," *American Anthropologist*, n.s., Vol. XVI (1914).

Howard, James H. "Pan-Indian Culture of Oklahoma," *Scientific Monthly*, Vol. LXXXI (November, 1955).

———, and Gertrude P. Kurath. "Ponca Dances, Ceremonies and Music," *Ethnomusicology*, Vol. II (1959).

Jablow, Joseph. "The Cheyenne in Plains Indian Trade Relations (1795–1840)," American Ethnological Society *Monographs*, No. 19. 1951.

Jenness, Diamond. "Indians of Canada," National Museum of Canada *Bulletin 65.* 1932.

———. "Sarcee Indians of Alberta," National Museum of Canada *Bulletin 90.* 1938.

Kinietz, Vernon. "Notes on the Roached Headdress of Animal Hair among the North American Indians," Michigan Academy of Science, Arts and Letters *Papers,* Vol. XXVI (1940).

Kroeber, Alfred L. "The Arapaho," American Museum of Natural History *Bulletin,* Vol. XVIII, Part 1 (1902).

———. "Ethnology of the Gros Ventre," American Museum of Natural History *Anthropological Papers,* Vol. I, Part 4 (1908).

Lowie, Robert H. "The Assiniboine," American Museum of Natural History *Anthropological Papers,* Vol. IV, Part 1 (1909).

———. "Societies of the Crow, Hidatsa and Mandan Indians," American Museum of Natural History *Anthropological Papers,* Vol. XI, Part 3 (1913).

———. "Dances and Societies of the Plains Shoshone," American Museum of Natural History *Anthropological Papers,* Vol. XI, Part 10 (1915).

———. "Sun Dance of the Crow Indians," American Museum of Natural History *Anthropological Papers,* Vol. XVI, Part 1 (1915).

———. "Societies of the Kiowa," American Museum of Natural History *Anthropological Papers,* Vol. XI, Part 11 (1916).

———. "Crow Indian Art," American Museum of Natural History *Anthropological Papers,* Vol. XXI, Part 4 (1922).

Lynd, James W. "The Religion of the Dakotas," Minnesota Historical Society *Collections,* Vol. II, Part 2 (1860).

Mandelbaum, D. G. "The Plains Cree," American Museum of Natural History *Anthropological Papers,* Vol. XXXVII (1940).

Marriott, Alice. "Ribbon Applique Work of North American Indians, Part I," Oklahoma Anthropological Society *Bulletin,* Vol. VI (March, 1958). Unfortunately, additional parts were never published.

McClintock, Walter. "Dances of the Blackfeet Indians," *Southwest Museum Leaflets,* No. 7. Los Angeles.

McGee, W. J. "Ponka Feather Symbolism," *American Anthropologist,* Vol. XI (1898).

Olsen, Stanley J. "Dating Early Plains Buttons by Their Form," *American Antiquity*, Vol. XXVIII, No. 4 (April, 1963).

Orchard, William C. "Beads and Beadwork of the American Indians," Museum of the American Indian *Contributions*, Vol. XI (1929).

———. "Technique of Porcupine Quill Decoration among the North American Indians," Museum of the American Indian *Contributions*, Vol. IV, No. 1 (1916).

Parsons, Elsie C. "Notes on the Caddo," American Anthropological Association *Memoirs*, No. 57 (1941).

Powell, Louis H. "A Study of Indian Beadwork of the North Central Plains," St. Paul (Minnesota) Science Museum *Indian Leaflets*, Nos. 5–7, 1953.

Skinner, Alanson B. "Societies of the Iowa, Kansa and Ponca Indians," American Museum of Natural History *Anthropological Papers*, Vol. XI, Part 9 (1915).

———. "Ethnology of the Ioway Indians," Milwaukee Public Museum *Bulletin*, Vol. V, No. 4 (1926).

Spinden, Herbert J. "The Nez Percé Indians," American Anthropological Association *Memoirs*, Vol. II (1908).

Steward, J. "Culture Element Distributions: Nevada Shoshone," University of California *Anthropological Records*, Vol. IV, No. 2 (1941).

Wedel, Waldo R. "Kansa Indians," Kansas Academy of Science *Transactions*, Vol. XLIX, No. 1 (1946).

Whitman, William. "The Oto," Columbia University *Contributions to Anthropology*, Vol. XXVIII (1937).

Wildschut, William, and John C. Ewers. "Crow Indian Beadwork," Museum of the American Indian *Contributions*, Vol. XVI. 1959.

Will, G. F., and Herbert J. Spinden. "The Mandans," Peabody Museum of American Archaeology and Ethnology *Harvard University Papers*, Vol. III, No. 4 (1906).

Wissler, Clark. "Costumes of the Plains Indians," American Museum of Natural History *Anthropological Papers*, Vol. XVII (1915).

———. "Distribution of Moccasin Decorations among the Plains Tribes," American Museum of Natural History *Anthropological Papers*, Vol. XXIX, Part 1 (1927).

———. "General Discussion of Shamanistic and Dancing Societies," American Museum of Natural History *Anthropological Papers*, Vol. XI, Part 12 (1916).

———. *Indian Beadwork*. American Museum of Natural History Guide Leaflet No. 50. New York, 1931.

———. *Indian Costumes in the United States*. American Museum of Natural History Guide Leaflet No. 63. New York, 1931.

———. "The Influence of the Horse in the Development of Plains Culture," *American Anthropologist*, n.s., Vol. XVI, No. 1 (January-March, 1914).

———"Material Culture of the Blackfoot Indians," American Museum of Natural History *Anthropological Papers*, Vol. V, Part 1 (1910).

———. "The Material Culture of North American Indians," *American Anthropologist*, n.s., Vol. XVI (1914).

———. *North American Indians of the Plains*. American Museum of Natural History, Handbook Series, No. 1. New York, 1912.

———. "Societies and Ceremonial Associations in the Oglala Division of the Teton-Dakota," American Museum of Natural History *Anthropological Papers*, Vol. XI, Part 1 (1912).

———. "Structural Basis to the Decoration of Costumes among the Plains Indians," American Museum of Natural History *Anthropological Papers*, Vol. XVII, Part 3 (1916).

Wood, W. Raymond. "Perforated Elk Teeth: A Functional and Historical Analysis," *American Antiquity*, Vol. XXII (1957).

Woods, C. A. "A Criticism of Wissler's North American Culture Areas," *American Anthropologist*, n.s., Vol. XXXVI (1934).

Woodward, Arthur. *Indian Trade Goods*. Portland, Oregon Archaeological Society, 1965.

References for the New and Advanced Hobbyist

American Indian Tradition (formerly *American Indian Hobbyist*).

Austin, Robert. "Fingerweaving," *Powwow Trails*, Vol. VI, No. 7 (1969).

Chandler, Milford G., and David A. Kracinski. "Unusual Beadwork Techniques, Part I," *American Indian Tradition*, Vol. VIII, No. 5 (1962).

Charnley, Donn. "Crow Loop Necklace," *American Indian Hobbyist,* Vol. V, Nos. 5, 6 (1959).

Conn, Richard. "Blackfoot Women's Clothing," *American Indian Hobbyist,* Vol. VII, No. 4 (1961).

———. "Braided Sashes," *American Indian Tradition,* Vol. IX, No. 1 (1963).

———. "Cheyenne Style Beadwork," *American Indian Tradition,* Vol. VII, No. 2 (1961).

———. "Northern Plains Bustles," *American Indian Tradition,* Vol. VII, No. 1 (1960).

———. "Western Sioux Beadwork," *American Indian Hobbyist,* Vol. VI, Nos. 9, 10 (1960).

Evans, Dennis. "Southern Plains Women's Boots," *American Indian Tradition,* Vol. VIII, No. 5 (1962).

Feder, Norman. "Bottom Tab Leggings," *American Indian Tradition,* Vol. VIII, No. 4 (1962).

———. "The Crow Indians of Montana," *American Indian Hobbyist,* Vol. V, Nos. 5, 6 (1959).

———. "Front Seam Leggings," *American Indian Tradition,* Vol. VIII, No. 3 (1962).

———. *Head and Tail Fans.* Somerset, New Jersey, Powwow Trails, 1965.

———. "Oklahoma Fancy Dance Costume," *American Indian Hobbyist,* Vol. IV, Nos. 5, 6 (1958).

———. "Otter Fur Turbans," *American Indian Tradition,* Vol. VII, No. 3 (1961).

———. "Plains Hair and Roach Ornaments," *American Indian Hobbyist,* Vol. IV, Nos. 9, 10 (1958).

———. "Plains Indian Metalworking," *American Indian Tradition,* Vol. VIII, Nos. 2, 3 (1962).

———. "Quill and Horsehair Feather Ornaments," *American Indian Hobbyist,* Vol. VI, Nos. 9, 10 (1960).

———. "Ribbon Applique," *American Indian Hobbyist,* Vol. III, Nos. 2, 3 (1956).

———. "Shoshone Split-Horn Bonnet," *American Indian Hobbyist,* Vol. VI, Nos. 3, 4 (1959).

————, and Milford G. Chandler. "Grizzly Claw Necklaces," *American Indian Tradition*, Vol. VIII, No. 1 (1961).

————, and Clyde Feltz. "Bustle Trailers," *American Indian Hobbyist*, Vol. III, Nos. 9, 10 (1957).

————, and ————. "Old Time Sioux Costume," *American Indian Hobbyist*, Vol. IV, Nos. 3, 4 (1957).

————, and ————. "Modern Plateau Dance Costume," *American Indian Hobbyist*, Vol. III, Nos. 9, 10 (1957).

Holm, Bill. "Making a Blanket 'Capote'," *American Indian Hobbyist*, Vol. III, No. 1 (1956).

————. "Plains Indian Cloth Dresses," *American Indian Hobbyist*, Vol. IV, Nos. 5, 6 (1958).

Howard, James H. "Northern Plains Grass Dance Costume," *American Indian Tradition*, Vol. VII, No. 1 (1960).

————. "The Roach Headdress," *American Indian Hobbyist*, Vol. VI, Nos. 7, 8 (1960).

Hunt, W. Ben. *Golden Book of Indian Crafts and Lore.* New York, Simon and Schuster, 1954.

Indian America (formerly *American Indian Crafts and Culture* and *The Singing Wire;* official newsletter for California Indian Hobbyists).

Jester, Margo. "Peace Medals," *American Indian Tradition*, Vol. VII, No. 5 (1961).

Johnson, Michael G. "Blackfoot Bonnet," *Powwow Trails*, Vol. II, No. 5 (1965).

————. "Indian Beadwork from the Canadian Plains," *Powwow Trails*, Vol. V, No. 10 (1969).

————"A Note on Indian Coats and Jackets," *Powwow Trails*, Vol. V, No. 8 (1969).

————. "Western Sioux Man's Costume, 1880–1910," *Powwow Trails*, Vol. VI, Nos. 1, 2 (1969).

Kracinski, David A. "Unusual Beadwork Techniques, Part II," *American Indian Tradition*, Vol. IX, No. 1 (1963).

LaQuay, E. "Beadwork," *Powwow Trails*, Vol. I, No. 6 (1964).

Little, Shan. "A Sioux Woman's Dentalium Shell Dress," *American Indian*

    Crafts and Culture, Vol. II, No. 10 (1968).

Mason, Bernard S. *The Book of Indian Crafts and Costumes.* New York, Ronald, 1946.

Powers, William K. "Feathers Costume," *Powwow Trails*, Vol. III, Nos. 7, 8 (1966).

————. *Grass Dance Costume.* Somerset, New Jersey, Powwow Trails, 1965.

————. *Here Is Your Hobby: Indian Dancing and Costumes.* New York, G. P. Putnam's Sons, 1966.

Powwow Trails.

Smith, Jerry. *Oklahoma Fancy Dance Outfit.* Panorama City, California Indian Hobbyist Association, 1968.

————. *Oklahoma Straight Dancer.* Panorama City, California Indian Hobbyist Association, n.d.

————. "Otter Drop," *American Indian Crafts and Culture.* Vol. II, No. 4 (1968).

————, and Randy Kroha. "Oklahoma Fancy Dancers, 1972," *American Indian Crafts and Culture*, Vol. VI, No. 5 (1972).

Spittal, William Guy. "Blackfeet Hair Ornament," *American Indian Hobbyist*, Vol. II, No. 8 (1956).

————. "Blackfeet Horned Headdress," *American Indian Hobbyist*, Vol. II, No. 8 (1956).

Stewart, Tyrone H., and Jerry Smith. *The Oklahoma Feather Dancer.* Tulsa, American Indian Crafts and Culture, 1973.

Talking Leaves, newsletter of the American Indianist Society (formerly the New England Indian Hobbyist Association).

Taylor, Colin. "Plains Indians' Leggings," *English Westerner's Brand Book.* Vol. III, No. 2 (1961).

————. The Plains Indian Shirt," *American Indian Hobbyist*, Vol. III, Nos. 7, 8 (1957).

Tucker, Michael S. *Old Time Sioux Dancers.* Panorama City, California, Tyrone H. Stewart, 1969.

Whispering Wind, publication of the Louisiana Indian Hobbyist Association.

Miscellaneous Sources

Conn, Richard G. "A Classification of Aboriginal North American Clothing." Master's thesis, University of Washington, 1955.

Martin, Evelyn M. "Analysis of Indian Ceremonial Costumes of Central Oklahoma." Master's thesis, University of Southern California, 1942.

Murdock, George P. *Ethnographic Bibliography of North America. Human Relations Area Files.* 3d Edition. New Haven, Yale University, 1960.

Smith, Jerry. "Oklahoma Straight Dancer," paper written for the California Indian Hobbyist Association ca. 1968.

Thorp, Rowena W. "The Dress of the Plains Indian Women and Children." Master's thesis, Southern Methodist University, 1935.

INDEX

215